SOM
journal

4

HATJE
CANTZ

Contents

Introduction

Diane Ghirardo

How does a large, established company remain fresh and relevant? Maintaining a high quality of work presents successors with problems, particularly when the leaders responsible for the company's once-great reputation retire. Corporations often become accustomed to doing things in the same way, which often leads to a rigidity that bodes ill for creativity, and diminishes the ability to tackle new issues. Instead, a corporation requires a mindset and an institutional structure distinctly flexible and unburdened by the weight of its own history. An institution's stasis can be furthermore exacerbated by their troubled hiring policies—as the general tendency is to hire and promote those who are similar in background and training, and who will not threaten power structures within the firm.

Institutional freshness is a vexing problem, but also an interesting one. When Wilfried Wang, editor of SOM Journals 1, 2, and 3, asked me to jury for projects from the various partnership offices in 2003, I was primarily intrigued by their decision to expose work from its offices to the evaluation of a jury over which the firm and its partners exerted no control. Their yield of control is best exemplified by their willingness to publish the jury's comments in their entirety. For its success, the SOM jury depends upon the firm's internal competitiveness emerging not only within the firm, but externally as well. Despite my initial reservations, I have found the whole process ably constructed to spark free discussion among the jurors. After holding the early juries in various SOM offices—which led to cries of foul from the offices whose projects were not selected—the partners elected to move the jury outside of the United States to sites not under the control of anyone in the partnership; first Berlin (for

Journal 3) and then Helsinki. Choosing jurors from several related fields (art, engineering, and criticism, and the practice) also encouraged an exchange of ideas rather than partisanship. Participating in the juries has led me to think about both how to measure and how to achieve good design, and it has also encouraged me to think about the life cycle of institutions.

The challenge of heading off staleness troubles many types of institutions: hiring graduates from the same schools ensures quality but eliminates the diversity and edge that can spring from bringing together people of different ages, backgrounds, and experiences. Most institutions find it difficult to accept that revitalization springs not from the comfortable center but from the uncomfortable margins. Short of hiring armies of new colleagues, how can an institution shake itself out of complacency? SOM has devised its own way of meeting this challenge, one that involves both internal discussion and external verification.

Professional corporations trade in profitability; their capital *is* capital, while other institutions, such as higher education, trade in cultural capital, something not measurable in dollars and cents but still easy to recognize. Because architecture is related to art, firms seek not simply business, but also reputation and cultural capital—recognition of accomplishment beyond the balance sheet. SOM aims to encourage profitability by making a claim on cultural capital in two ways: raising the quality of design through internal competition, and publishing the jury-selected projects (with juror comments) in an externally-received journal. Their aim here is not to produce the vanity coffee-table book. In effect, the mere willingness to open itself, to seek out external criticism is itself a form of cultural capital. Certainly no other firms have done so in the past. None are prepared to follow in SOM's steps by instituting their own independent juries and publications.

Undergoing public external review is not new terrain for architects; designs and buildings undergo almost constant evaluation—by the public, by the critics, by other architects, and by its users. Architects become accustomed to the criticism process early in their careers—as students they undergo bi-semester public juries, even if only other architects serve on them. Professional organizations such as the AIA regularly review and reward projects, and in these cases the evaluation becomes more explicit, although again the jurors are other architects. Once an architect joins a firm, the judging is usually largely informal and predicated on the responses of clients. In some respects, nothing could be more familiar to architects than the jury process and competition with other architects. What is unusual about the SOM competition is that they initiate a jury process unrelated to the client response, and take this jury outside of the firm.

The general perception of SOM is that the firm was at the cutting edge of architecture from the 1950s to the 1970s; in recent years it has not maintained that edge. I personally associated the firm with stock skyscrapers and little else. My first turn on the jury in 2003 brought to light a firm engaged in a far richer array of buildings and in some cases, of a caliber unexpectedly higher than anticipated. I was surprised by many things, such as a palette of seductive and elegant textures in a firm I had dismissed as indifferently corporate. The projects documented in *Journal 4* illustrate architectural designs of remarkable quality, at times achieving poetry comparable to the best I have seen.

But not all projects submitted to the jury reflected that high level of quality. Three unfavorable qualities were especially notable. In both of my turns on the jury, I was appalled at the designs which evinced complete indifference to their contexts. This indifference is something I expect to see in the work of a third- or fourth-year architecture student, but not of a solid professional office. This indifference often went hand-in-hand with the trivializing adoption of metaphors as faux-design triggers, especially apparent in projects destined for cultures outside of the United States and Western Europe. Finally, I was also dismayed to see how little attention most projects gave to environmental issues, to questions of sustainable resources and "green" design more generally. Knowing what we do today about the state of the environment, it is unforgivable that any firm would not make such concerns a fundamental feature of *every* project. It is not enough to say that clients are reluctant, or that upfront costs are too great. To my mind insisting upon this as a fundamental feature of every project is nothing short of a moral imperative. Vast expanses of glass in climates and locations that can ill-support such expensive buildings vexed me profoundly. Since SOM has now taken a leadership role in confronting the challenges of corporate architecture, perhaps the firm will also take on the challenge of environmentally sensitive design.

With those significant reservations in mind, let me turn to the jury process. Through the juror and architect Juhani Pallasmaa, we were able to hold the jury in Alvar Aalto's studio—a setting at once invigorating and daunting for all concerned, not least the projects being reviewed. As a group, we were pleased with both the quality and the range of projects we selected—from a skyscraper to a restoration project to a joint for a structural system. Our goal was to reduce the number of designs to five; coming in at six, we very nearly made it. But we had to leave behind some terrific projects, including a personal favorite of mine, the façade for ABC Studios, on State Street in Chicago, which engaged the public expression of a contemporary media conglomerate in a refreshingly clear and inventive fashion. Nonetheless, the jury was satisfied that the most thoughtful and inventive work had emerged. Best of all, reviewing the projects gave us the opportunity to discuss architecture in an evocative environment. In our summation, we emphasized that several of the projects embodied critical engagement with issues such as degraded urban environments, pristine landscapes, restoration of modern architecture and structural innovation, all concerns remarkably and broadly present in SOM's offices. We also lauded the clarity and depth of the presentations of these particular designs. The limitations were identical for all, yet not every design could be deciphered, largely because of confusing or incomplete presentations.

Pin-Fuse Joint™

As demonstrated in recent disasters, architects and engineers face ever greater challenges in seismic design. For a firm that built its reputation on skyscrapers, nothing could be more appropriate than to confront the engineering issues that earthquakes pose to tall buildings. Even though designers have come up with ways for steel frame structures to yield to seismic forces without collapsing, the resultant deformations added significant costs to post-earthquake repairs. SOM's answer is a Pin-Fuse Joint™ engineered to allow a connection between beam and column to slip while maintaining elasticity, thereby avoiding the high costs associated with restoring structural integrity to a building. The resultant joint, so deceptively simple, illustrates the merits of research in an architectural firm. Designing skyscrapers along the Pacific Rim (also known as the "Ring of Fire" for its high seismic activity) put the problem of the structural frame and its response to high seismic loads at the center of attention. SOM encouraged research whose results are directly applicable to the firm's activities, an approach the jury found particularly compelling and rewarding.

United States Air Force Academy Cadet Chapel Restoration

One of the most vexing problems that face contemporary preservationists is how to restore modern buildings, which degrade more rapidly than buildings centuries old. During early modernism's period of high enthusiasm, architects eagerly experimented with new materials. Unfortunately, the glues, vinyls, and plastics that generated such high optimism one-half century ago have not withstood the test of time: just try to match those asbestos-laced vinyl tiles today! One of the icons of modernism in the United States, SOM's Air Force Academy in Colorado, suffered problems associated with its enclosure almost from the outset. One year after completion, leaky aluminum joints had to be treated with a urethane sealant; incongruous gutters and downspouts were also added later to the famous tetrahedral aluminum frames. Over the ensuing forty years, the repeated use of the urethane sealant progressively discolored the aluminum panels. The commission to restore the structure's aesthetic and functional integrity allowed SOM to incorporate better performing materials such as silicone sheets, and to design a new weather barrier beneath the aluminum panels, in effect regaining structural integrity while maintaining the building's distinctive profile. There is relatively little attention devoted to the preservation of modern architecture, and in this case, SOM has responded with an exemplary restoration project. For the jury, having SOM go back and "get it right" signals a positive direction.

Creative and Performing Arts High School

SOM has carved out a unique and important specialization in the field of education, well illustrated by the project for the Camden Creative and Performing Arts High School. A magnet public school for talented students of dance, music, painting, sculpture, film, and other media, the school is situated in an area that is becoming an educational hub, with two charter schools and three higher education institutions nearby. Despite the abundance of schools, this part of Camden is neither prosperous nor well developed. Like many downtowns in the United States, Camden has suffered from the scorched earth of urban renewal—big box stores and the flight to the suburbs. That the city would have the courage to construct a school for the most artistically talented students demonstrates a strong faith in the city's future, a vision SOM embraced and to which its design gives body. Building up one end of the site and leaving a grassy play space adjacent to the building emphasizes the project's public character by giving a green space inside a dense urban core. Programmatic requirements guide the adjustments to the building's modular frame, grouping and dispersing spaces and disrupting the elevations in irregular and exuberant patterns. The jury responded especially to this project's expansiveness, as it quite literally reaches out to the city with its ebullient façades, vibrant colors and textures, and walls that open fully to the outdoors. The school declares itself to be unabashedly public, a modernist building unusually engaged and responsive to its surroundings.

Schloss Velden

A luxury spa on a pristine site does not resonate as a socially ambitious project, yet the jury found the solution proposed for this area in Austria to be subtle and ingenious, an object lesson in how to enhance rather than overpower the existing environment. Schloss Velden earned praise also because it was a rarity among the designs we reviewed, with its attention to energy efficiency and sustainability. The old Schloss remains the iconic structure in the new spa, adjacent to which the architects produced a landscape of folded and undulating grassy terraces. Diverse rooms and facilities are tucked into their folds. The project is so unique and its components so distinctive, that room plans differ: entry into each room triggers new experiences and discoveries. In its deceptive simplicity, the design actually embraces an artful complexity that became more intriguing the more the jury studied it. Although the design team described the design as organic, it is only so from a bird's eye view; from the ground up, it is sinuous and rational. Additionally notable was the attention to issues of sustainability, visual as well as environmental.

West Bay Office Tower

Of the many skyscraper projects the jury reviewed, we selected the West Bay Office Tower for Doha, Qatar, as the most representative and original. Whatever the jurors thought of skyscrapers—and the building type only had a couple of partisans—we all agreed that West Bay embodied the best of SOM's skyscraper designs this year. Located in a high-rise area of Qatar overlooking the Persian Gulf, this design proposes to be environmentally sensitive both through sunshades and by positioning the offices differently depending upon solar orientation. While we had no documentation on precisely how the building operates in the hot desert climate, the attention the designers paid to environmental issues persuaded us that such concerns lay behind the design itself, and that it

appears likely to succeed. Although the panels illustrated images of desert sands and satellite photographs of the port area, the project treated the surroundings as a flat plain. Despite this, the development of the structural cage struck the jury with its elegant stone cladding arrayed as delicate diagonal braces. Contrary to expectations, the bracing both thins and densifies as it soars to the top, the last of a series of sophisticated layers. Once again, a remarkably complicated structure was designed with such stunning simplicity that even the jurors not fond of skyscrapers were persuaded.

ARB Bank Headquarters

ARB Bank was one of the two most unusual projects the jury selected. With its monolithic rammed earth walls and low profile tucked into a series of ramps, the dusky structure rises from an agricultural landscape with which it is both allied and set apart. Walls fabricated of local earth sympathize with their surroundings, but the cubic form is distinctly alien to the shifting and sinuous local dunes. Inside, the structure contains the most advanced technologies deployed within a series of interlocking L-shaped tiers; outside, it employs one of the most ancient building systems. This juncture of high and primitive technologies is a fascinating concept, and here the two are joined seamlessly to gain the assets of both: the thermal barrier uses cheap local materials, while the steel and glass interiors make it possible to intersperse open spaces within the interlocking L blocks. The construction system dictates the project's aesthetics, a fact that helped the design to receive high marks from the jury. But even beyond that, the periscope windows, almost medieval in the way they penetrate the earthen walls, lift the project to a level of poetry of the highest order.

Tim Macfarlane, Carlos Jimenez, Diane Ghirardo, Juhani Pallasmaa, and Petra Blaisse during the jury review at the Alvar Aalto Studio

Jury Transcript

Diane Ghirardo, Petra Blaisse, Carlos Jimenez, Tim Macfarlane, Juhani Pallasmaa

June 27, 2004
Helsinki, Finland

Diane Ghirado First, we are looking at the **Nanjing Guozi-Greenland Financial Mansion**. Any comments that we would like to make?

Carlos Jimenez I was surprised, being such a major project, at how little information there was on it. That was surprising for such a large project.

Juhani Pallasmaa I would like to understand the idea of the design and visual intention this building; I can't quite get it. Can you or anyone explain what these images mean?

Tim Macfarlane There's a little concept statement here that discusses where the different elements come from, but then there's no development visible here on the board. So it seems a very superficial gesture, to arrive at what was a very slick image of a tower.

Petra Blaisse It talks about natural forces—about wind and water and so on. But it doesn't really translate in anything comprehensible, why, what, where? And then it makes clear that it's about two different buildings. Both with so many square meters of office, hotel, retail, residential. So I understand there's a low block and a high-rise and they have a connection with a glass bridge. That's as far as it goes, basically. Apart from form.

DG And even if the form is elegant, that doesn't quite make up for the rest.

PB You have no idea about the plans, the organization, the movement.

JP And what is this skeleton structure? Are they movement patterns or what are they?

CJ Circulation patterns, vertical circulation patterns.

DG It says, "The tower has been derived from the three elements of life in Nanjing Yangtze River: lush green landscape and the dragon and column iconography."

DG And?

PB Those are three things.

DG And I'm having trouble with finding all of them in it. Although, in certain ways, this is an elegant tower, it's an elegant form. It's not enough. So—any votes for this?

PB I don't find it interesting.

DG Project 2 is the **Beijing New Vision International Exhibition Center.**

PB Do you know where it's located? I can't see any context.

DG There's a short description here that talks about the location.

CJ Actually, most of these projects in China, they seem to be almost without a context. They are so placeless.

DG That's more of a general remark, don't you think?

CJ Yes, yes, it's more general. But there's just the usual suspect buildings in the background.

JP But that's the character of Beijing today. There are thousands of isolated buildings, but they don't create any kind of a city sense.

DG And so what you're arguing is that this project doesn't really offer anything to combat that tendency.

JP My comment was a general comment. I'm not sure of this case, but it's a very clear scheme. I understand what it is about.

TM I find it quite retro, the whole structural expression here is very '60s.

CJ It was the space frame convention centers that were done from Chicago to the end of the world.

DG There are certain things that I like in this set of textures. I quite like the colors and the materials. I thought that they were nicely represented, actually, but they're bits and pieces. They don't really add up. This is a case where there's an insertion of a view of the traditional environment that one assumes is somewhere nearby, but it's not clear; and then what's the relationship of this part to that one? In other words, is this image here to enhance the project? Is it here to say, "This is the way it looks now with these wonderful pale lights and this low

Alvar Aalto Studio, Helsinki, Finland, 2002

topography," and what's the relationship to this?

CJ Well, I think it's to suggest the idea that the buildings, like convention centers, are now—this idea of attracting light, generating light.

DG But does this sort of image do it?

TM If you look at the description at the top here, they talk about the "Forbidden City unfolds in a sequence of towering walled courtyards and gardens illuminated by softly glowing lanterns," so it's sort of this idea of having the walled city underneath the great canopy. But it's very difficult to know what other

references give it any backbone or strength. It's very arbitrary on these boards as to how you might arrive at any of the elements. And, as I say, I think the roof is very out of time.

PB Well, I think it's more—if I may be a bit harsher than all of you. It's a kind of cliché—referring to scale and atmosphere that you don't recognize in any way in what you're seeing in the new building. So it's a bundle of clichés put together and I think it's not an attractive plan in that sense. You don't know where it is; the Forbidden City and all the things they describe as so subtle and so beautiful

and so well organized in scale and composition and then you see kind of indeed '70s, '80s collage—

CJ Well, it's very heavy-handed, this work.

PB Yes, even the interior. I understand what you mean, but it's like the sentimental cliché reference to beautiful Chinese things, that don't show anywhere how it's used, where and why. It's, again, a cliché interior with an atrium and a water piece. I would say forget it.

DG Okay. Number three is the **Dalian Futures and Commodities Exchange.** Now this is a skyscraper project, this is one of several, actually.

CJ It's an imperial park.

PB So what do you think?

JP Well, I have difficulties with skyscrapers as a building type. I don't seem to understand it, so you have to speak for it.

PB Well, that's more a general comment that we might have here as well. That a skyscraper, in some people's views, is interesting if you know why it's a skyscraper and how movement occurs through a high-rise building within a context of a city or a flat plain. You have to understand that before you can appreciate it, otherwise, they all become landmarks.

Beijing New Vision International Exhibition Center

Dalian Futures and Commodities Exchange

JP Yes. And, as a building type, I think it's a kind of a package. You are packaging your office or hotel or wherever space and then the architectural form is reduced to how you decorate that package.

PB These are actually more interesting than you would have thought. This is hanging, floating within a frame, it's totally transparent.

CJ What's interesting in this project is the way that it's not only a vertical solution in terms of dividing of the square footage, but it's also a horizontal solution. You know, the way that it begins to create these rings and ground planes that contrast quite well with the verticality. It's an unusual scheme, in a sense, like the John Hancock Tower, you made reference to this, it's a singular object, isolated, almost iconic and here there's more a sense of understanding the horizontal tissue of the skyscraper's past.

PB But do you understand it?

CJ No, but formally, I like very much the way that it creates a precinct, a domain instead of just being an overwhelming vertical image.

TM I think with high-rise buildings it's important how they hit the ground and how they kind of engage with everything in the vicinity. And it's very hard to know what we're shown here and what sort of texture you had there before you suddenly have this enormous plaza development.

DG Right. And we may want to not vote yes or no on this, but hold this for the moment. There is this effort in this project to deal with the ground plaza, which hasn't been common in the past. There is a kind of elegance to this solution that may be, in some respects, dated, but sometimes dated things are okay when they're elegant enough.

PB My hesitation is that, here is this beautiful image. I'm not sentimental about old at all, but can you imagine how you walk here and what you experience and then, all of a sudden—I wonder how you experience this? Also, as you see, the sketch is about the block itself, but the whole connection with the rest is—you can always make an axis anywhere, but it doesn't say there's any logic here. Do you see why the axis would go like this? It goes right through a tower.

CJ Well, it's like you go to a gate, like a gateway.

DG This is the ocean and the river, so I have this feeling that your principal direction's going to be that way and you're going to be coming back from there, but you're mostly going perhaps to the seaside, but I'm not sure. You're also looking from here outward with it, so that might be quite nice. I like seeing this drawing here, because it gives evidence that they've thought about it.

PB And what the views everywhere would be.

DG We'll hold this in for the moment. Next, this is the **Midwest Bank Branch Prototype**; number four, in Missouri. I think the first bank here was done by Bruce Graham.

PB That's nice. That's very nice.

TM Help me understand. This prototype, now, has it—

CJ It's almost a generic, 5000-square-foot branch prototype. Which would be placed anywhere in the Midwest. That's why the images are placed in these generic fields, as you see. These are highway banks.

TM You do see that it doesn't seem to have shifted much since Bruce Graham's idea. They have total respect for Bruce Graham's idea.

PB It says here the project "comments on the changes of the historical model of the banking typology and its representation of banking. The historic model of the classical façade that mystically participated in the village center spoke to the idea of projecting

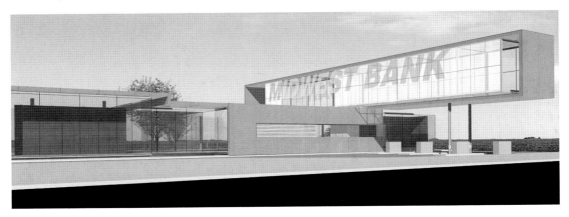

Midwest Bank Branch Prototype

security, strength and conservative fiscal values."

DG Banks like this are 19th-century inventions, though banks existed before, they weren't about places and spaces. They were people and repositories of money and stands in plazas, but not buildings. These are very much 19th-century structures.

TM Is this coming from Bruce Graham's original approach to the problem or is it referring to this kind of design?

PB The design is supposed to be a comment on the whole evolution and history of banking.

TM So is this a drive-in bank? Do you whiz through here and put your card in the box?

CJ This is a really old bank. It announces its function along the freeway or the highway.

PB It looks like it could be—all the volumes have a different role, so you have drive-in, you have maybe advisory on how you could invest, and human communication in this block, for instance. And, at the same time, it advertises for the bank in general.

CJ You see the vault, you see the signage, enter here, exit. The part that is not clear is this model. It's really—it's just a thick billboard ring.

TM I think that's the flower scheme.

CJ A network of banking transactions, I guess, changing and shifting. And the nature of the Midwest.

JP Somehow it appears old-fashioned to me. It speaks of the banking of the '60s, perhaps, but not today's electronic digital banking at all.

TM Also, I think the trouble with America, with the prototype for the Americas, if you're looking at things like diversity of the climates, I mean, even in the Midwest, you'd probably do from north to south, the Midwest includes all those latitudes there.

DG That's an early conceptual diagram, I thought. Treated like a painting and actually it's quite nice. But then there is the translation from that into the structure of the landscape. I have to say, in terms of the way this might fit into the Midwest sort of strip-center model, I think it will fit just fine, but I also don't think that it adds anything particularly interesting or new or makes it more elegant than anything that's already there. So I see it as an environmental problem, quite significantly, with all of the glazing.

PB What is nicely symbolized also is the digital era. You can have electronic transferrals, weightless banking, there's no collection of gold ingots. So it's all very light, feather-light, it's quick.

CJ We designed a bank like this, but the biggest complaint we got was from the tellers saying there was too much light and they couldn't see, because of the digital text that you read.

DG Right. That's the problem with half the ATM machines that you encounter, it's true.

PB So you would like to understand more about these kind of things.

DG In other words, if this is the type, are there variations on the type and what would the variations be for different environments?

TM I think it's specific and it's very site-specific.

CJ There is no denying there is a design talent or there's a composition. But if we're going to talk about it at length, we should know more those aspects of this generic quality. Because that is the merit of a prototype, that it can be adaptable anywhere and yet what are the mechanics of the orientation.

PB Yes. What I would like to know is what the budget is. And whether it's prefab and how you transport it and, you know, all these things because if it's really cheap and if you can really manipulate it in many ways, it becomes much more interesting.

CJ But also the more generic, the more efficient, because you're eliminating the idea that the design is so specific. It has to be almost like a box or a very generic floor plan, but this is highly specific. That's the mystery—because the moment you speak about prototyping, you're talking about transformation, adaptability....

DG Okay. So we'll leave it for the moment. **John Jay College of Criminal Justice** in New York

CJ I think the cross-section of these buildings is the most interesting thing about the project—it's unifying the existing building with a new one.

TM Actually, it was extended, wasn't it? John Jay was extended. Let's see what it says. That was the first extension that was done by Viñoly.

CJ It's unifying both the projects—tying the two together, isn't it?

TM Yes, it's tying that one to that one and getting the frontage to 12th Avenue on a very steep hill up 57th and 58th Streets.

JP Well, there's a lack of scale; it's just huge and it doesn't give any human measure.

CJ No measure of space.

JP Yes, I can't relate myself to the building in terms of scale. To me, its scale is both outside and inside.

PB I think you really do see scale, in the floorplans and in entrances, and also in comparison to other buildings here. And what I like is this is the first time (or one of the few times) I really understand the given program in this way.

JP I experience it as a person in relation to the huge thing without any mediation. I would like to have a mediation from my scale to the scale of the structure.

DG I actually think it does that. Although there are things about this entranceway that I'm not happy with, I don't understand how that transition takes place. It is too abrupt, too unclear. But there is a transition in scale. There are places that you're able to move to and see yourself in relation to different levels of the building. But I believe there must be—because it's a College of Criminal Justice, there must be labs. There must be all sorts of facilities to undertake different types of research and to understand different aspects of criminology. So I wish I understood more about the relationship of classrooms to labs to circulation; I think the information is probably there, I just can't read it.

TM They say that this is an all-glass building, of course, whose programmatic function is to lead in the exterior demonstrating the transparency of justice.

PB But there is no transparency.

TM I mean, there's multiple arguments about this whole paradox of glass as a transparency. Even the idea of the façade working technically to bring light into the building, so that you have daylight rather than electric light and what that means in energy terms, what that means in comfort terms, what that means from an emotional point of view. And they are all, to me, things that should guide how this façade is developed and how long it's been treated in many ways on this elevation—in a suggestion that's cluttering the portal.

CJ It's surprising that there's no indication of detail at all of the wall system, the window wall system. It's absent.

JP Yes, I would wish the building to express its typological essence, that it is a school, an educational building. I don't see that at all. It speaks of a secular working space rather than an educational community.

DG One can imagine that this could be developed in such a way that it would accomplish all of the things that you have been talking about. But we're just not told how that happens or that that's even a consideration in the development of this project.

TM That's right. And in the language here, I mean, it talks about how the cascade acts as an organized program where it

maximizes natural light in; and so there is a discussion about light, but that's the only discussion.

DG This is another case where the choice of what's represented and how it's represented doesn't help sell the project to us. For example, when I look at this, it looks quite nice, but I'm not sure that that's as important to me as some of this would have been at a larger scale so I could make sense of it or some detailed elaboration of the skin.

PB What irritates me, and that's also a general remark, is that the description doesn't match what they actually do. It's all beautiful about the cascade connecting, but, actually, the cascade is only on limited levels, so you don't know how you move through and why they are towers. And I think, from

John Jay College of Criminal Justice

outside, you don't see any programmatic difference.

TM Also, there's an extraordinary amount of space here which seems to be communicating between the two buildings, that whole area.

DG Well, I'm wondering what would make this space something other than just tedious.

TM Yes, I hate to use a reference, but this worked at the IIT, but going into that space, there's a whole vista of different things happening, but immediately within your eyesight, so you immediately walk into this true interest. Whereas you can see within here that there's light coming through, but again, there's no real complexity of interest described.

PB No, and there's no transparency to the spaces that will actually be used. First of all, there's no usable space in this enormous area.

TM It's like a tunnel.

PB So, actually, it's just nothing there.

DG No, although I think there's a number of interesting things about the project, and I think that we're happy about certain aspects of the presentation, but there's a level of development—this could be any nondescript building, so they have to put the name "John Jay College" on it to say, "This is a college," by contrast with a corporate office building. Maybe it says something about the state of colleges today that we're making these interchangeable in the United States, but nonetheless, I think we're saying maybe that's not the best solution.

CJ Well, there is a non-attentiveness in this design even in the signage, the fact that they didn't conceive of a way of not crossing the letters with structure here; that applies also to their treatment of the façade, that it seems totally inconsequential to the vitality that it professes to have inside. And I think it's—again, that's why this image is so perplexing. That they're really after more

of this almost longitudinal image, but then when you have to have this kind of blatant opportunism, you wonder why.

PB There is a kind of, if I may say it, laziness in this project. There are all beginnings and references, but there's no real going into the work. There's no real going further than the first step of composing and connecting and light.

JP I agree that it's aesthetically quite pleasing, however, it appears to be rather arbitrary, it's not generated by a functional pattern of any sort.

DG Well, if it is, we don't know what it is, we're not seeing it.

JP There is a kind of suffocation with this huge volume.

DG In or out?

PB I would say out.

DG Okay, the **Hirshhorn Museum and Sculpture Garden** in Washington, DC.

CJ What is the project about? Is it the building there?

DG This is the existing building. And this is the addition of a series of satellites. A café, a shop, and then this entry security segment are being added to the existing museum.

PB Café and shops. That's where you move first.

TM It's hard to see on the drawings as

well what exists and which are the proposal; they're just not given. It's hard to see where the line is. Well, it's hard to see the new work.

CJ And I don't understand why they need to replicate the same iconic image.

TM Well, respect for it. What you can see, though, is that it has an aura of being like a very solid exterior with a very specific voice. I mean, I agree, when I looked at it first, I thought—visually, it didn't attract me. But then I began to look at it a little bit more closely and I thought, well, it has definitely got some ideas there. The idea of this internal fenestration—there's probably a shape inside. I'd love to know what was on the front of that wall.

CJ And most of the circulation happens around the inner ring.

TM I think it's a little bit Guggenheim.

DG So the question I asked myself is, how do you add to something that already has this iconic, definitive, absolute shape? And even though I see that—your point that it's overly respectful, I'm not sure that I can imagine much one can do on the Mall in DC other than something that adds more pods to this thing at a smaller scale. I think this is a really tough problem. And I'm not sure that this isn't a pretty good solution here. I don't have

Hirshhorn Museum and Sculpture Garden

enough understanding of how this has developed to know whether it's a great solution. To me, it's still too schematic, because we had trouble figuring out exactly what this was.

CJ Yes, I just find it odd, because, first of all, the shape is so iconic, as you mentioned. And then there are the four legs, the four major structural connection points and then that, perhaps, there could have been another level of imagination here. Why does the shop and the café and the security entry have the same shape? It's essentially done already.

JP I actually first understood this as being the level below this, which possibly could have been another solution.

DG But you have to have the entrance. I mean, because of the security requirements now and all of the things that people have to go through to enter public spaces in the United States.

JP It seems to be elevated from the street level anyway.

PB Security setbacks.

CJ And I guess my main objection is that, when you have such an iconic building whether we like it or dislike it, it is a major force in the landscape. And then it could elicit a more imaginative solution. I mean, I imagine a café or shop that could

partake of this curve, but maybe it doesn't have to emulate it.

DG But I also think there's some other issues here which probably aren't included. I think there's inadequate presentation of the project, but anything that's built on the Mall in Washington, DC, and anything that's changed there goes through massive bureaucracies. Not to say that garbage doesn't get through, but I think that there's huge limitations which we're not being told about here that may have imposed serious limitations on what they could really do.

JP And then there is the legacy of the Hirshhorn. They are showing a drawing of the original scheme in order to suggest a geometry that is in accordance with the existing building.

DG Well, did he originally propose that?

JP Apparently, this is the original proposal. But, forty-whatever years later, I'm surprised that no one has come up with an equally brave solution of our time. I actually have a fondness for this building. It's a bunker, but it's a bunker that is rather friendly once you get inside the donut. But it's not an image that should be replicated, and, consequently trivialized. That solution of making a plinth would go a long way to resolve the

functional problems of the donut as an exhibition space.

DG And now we have the **GSA Headquarters** in Washington, DC.

PB Vertical garden.

CJ Very sustainable project.

DG This is another remodel. This is one of the types that are being addressed, a remodel of an existing building, either additions or—in this case, this is both an addition and a massive remodeling, in certain respects.

CJ But it's retrofitting it, too. Because the original building is still intact. So they're retrofitting the courtyards and the scheme is really powerful as an environmental fixture.

The GSA is the largest builder in the United States.

DG All of the courthouses, the post offices, all the federal buildings in the United States have to go through the GSA.

JP I guess it makes sense on a rational level, but it seems to be fairly schematic in the end.

DG Apart from this part here.

JP Yes, it hasn't become architecture yet.

CJ This is the most interesting part of it. It could have more of a sense of what it does. How it captures water, rain, but

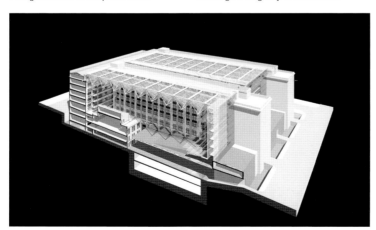

GSA Headquarters

there is a passivity in the way it's retained and—within the scale of the original building. But one wishes that this was really like something that is breathing, something that has the capacity to break from the box, you know? And maybe it is required, there's obviously cost issues around it, but I think there could be more imagination given to that.

PB Does anyone know what the program is for these huge volumes? What do they want to do?

CJ Well, it's creating a sustainable environment in a historical structure, so this becomes almost a model.

PB So it's a service to the original building of 1917.

DG Right. So how can you retrofit the building so that it becomes more sustainable? How can you deal with heat, light, water, all of these things through some form of retrofitting? The solution here is to bridge three different wings and to produce these courtyard spaces between them.

PB But the volume is twice as much as the original building, so you create these enormous volumes to economize heating costs and so on in the old building.

DG Yes. There are spaces for those who work there. They really are green-houses.

JP There's not sufficient indication of how the spaces would actually be used.

DG I think that they only tell us what this building might be. But one could imagine there would be facilities for meals and so on. And don't forget, Washington has a very inhospitable climate most of the year, whether from heat or cold, so this could be a place where people can go on lunch hours and breaks and so on and so forth. I would imagine that, if you're working on projects or you're having small meetings, you could go outside of these rather dark and relatively gloomy spaces and meet in the open area. Well, they really haven't developed

that here. I think the attention has been paid to how you can make the building sustainable. I think they've put their design attention and their thoughts on that rather than thinking about these spaces and how they're going to work afterwards.

PB And I can imagine that they want all the offices or spaces to look into the real exterior space and, on one side, into a kind of synthetic garden. That's why it's so high, I suppose. Because, if you look at it, it's not overwhelming the existing building, so why would they do it this way? It's too theoretic. It looks like a diagram of what the program wants, but what you should not do, in the end.

CJ This section suggests that water is used to balance heat differences. The water could have been made into something attractive and not just hidden in the basement.

DG So it doesn't have to be so formally aggressive. It could incorporate these elements and maybe then would become a part of this living tissue, as it were.

CJ I wouldn't say it's purely a formal solution. It's more a matter of programming, too. What happens in these volumes? Why not have water in one? Why not have a wild forest in the other

one? So one could begin to distinguish that these rooms are special within these three wings. I think it's the lack of program more than of form.

JP I could also think of how to use this immense wall in terms of height. Remember Paul Nelson's Suspended House project of 1939? The structure could be suspended and the space could be occupied somehow.

CJ I think of some of the new sustainable solutions. And then they create spaces that no one wants to be inside. I don't know if this is going to be as pleasant—a giant atrium from the '70s, remember those giant atriums? Wouldn't it be interesting if one of these things maybe has to be higher because it creates a flow of air or maybe one of them has to be lower, or something that gives them variation.

DG Okay, so should we keep this for the moment?

TM No, I wouldn't.

DG Actually, I would, because I have certain agendas, and one of them is that this sort of issue [environmental sustainability] be addressed in existing buildings. I wish this were a more compelling response to that question, but I'm not prepared to toss it out yet. We can go back to look at it, but I did think that was important.

Next, this is affordable urban housing in **Mount Vernon Square**. Well, there's a range. Some are for people with incomes under $47,000 a year, and there are both rental and sale units.

CJ You know, I thought this program was quite interesting, because I hadn't seen a drawing like this in a long time, this hand drawing. But, then, when you see it later develop into this mega-formulation of images, it's a whole different world completely. I was just commenting more on the drawing. This is mixed use, multi-use, multiplex use.

PB That's nice. It has things sticking out and balconies created and has a kind of human scale of use view.

DG I wish I had some floor plans of individual units.

JP Yes, that's what I would like to see.

DG There are some things that I really quite like about this, which Petra just pointed out. I like some of those things. I like the materials and so forth. One of the things that I would always expect, if I'm going to see an apartment block with

rental and sale units that are as big as these apartments are, how many of them are there, what the average floor plan would be.

PB The quality of a building is the floor plan, and we don't see it.

CJ But it is problematic, when you see a building presented solely from the outside, a building that is about residential housing. When it's presented solely from an outside experience.

PB A very generic—I mean, it's hand-drawn, fine, but it's the most generic, cheap—

CJ That's right.

DG This is about affordable urban housing, communities, diversity, they have all these great things. Neighborhood-centered? This looks like a generic—you know, something that you have to walk through to get where you want to go, not something that you want to go through.

PB The illusion of this garden, well, romantic side lots.

DG I always ask myself, "Why do I like walking up this street and not on this street?" These are questions that they're not asking themselves here. When you see people always walking, people

congregating on certain streets, there are reasons for that.

CJ We know that one of the dilemmas that this project opens up is this question always of residences and transparency. Is this the only solution? You know, this mathematical multiplication of the same window; because we tend to feel that these kinds of spaces are fantastic to live in, but they're also very open, very un-private. Put up curtains or mini-blinds … how do you subdivide or how do you protect yourself?

DG So this is out.

PB Yes.

DG Okay. We have the **Tokyo Midtown Roppongi.**

CJ I have to say that I visited this whole complex. It's a mess. I find it slightly suspect when there are so many details on textural fabrics around. Because they're saying that each of these façades is derived from the solar studies?

PB It's the best part. It's the most beautiful. It's about shadows and that's very nice. But I miss, on this project, what the program is, what the given program is. Why do they make all these buildings, what is to be in it?

Mount Vernon Square

Tokyo Midtown Roppongi

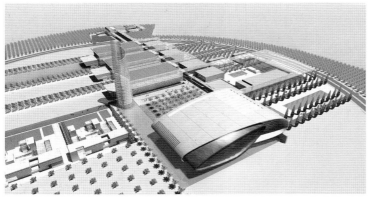

Bridging the Rift Foundation

DG It's a five-million-square-foot mixed-use development located in central Tokyo, where land values are astronomical. The project will include three commercial office and three residential buildings.

TM We have to move on ... to **Bridging the Rift Foundation.**

JP I would expect the "circle" to be somewhat reflected in the design itself. But there is no evidence of this.

TM It seems a very hard and sterile development and it seems that it would feel uncomfortable to be there.

PB There are also families, I read. So people really have to be there for a while.

CJ I wonder why the road couldn't have existed in another way. I wonder if the radiality of the design justifies this expanse.

TM Yes, it creates this problem of landscape and the idea that you've encircled it, but you haven't actually dealt with it. And, then, when you deal with it, you get these very formal gestures, which would be highly claustrophobic for me, I think.

CJ Well, I think they at least are making an effort to create on a certain issue of scale, but then you're going to have this emptiness. There's something peculiar and almost perverse about this very

formal gesture in the desert that negates where you are when you look at it. I like the suggestion that even the ring of vegetation is created, like an oasis that's always surrounding this element of nature. But, then here, the vegetation, it's curious. It's all very formal; it's like a yin-yang of vegetation.

PB It doesn't create a better environment for the people living there, it seems. No shade. It's not a roof or anything. But it does have a water system that is indigenous. "Indigenous plantings requiring minimal irrigational ... that provide further shade. Most importantly, in the ... oasis, water is strategically used not only to provide evaporative cooling and relieve the sense of oppressive heat, but to enhance the spatial focus of the center and reinforce connections between function, space, and people." I don't see the water connecting anything yet.

CJ This could be water, all of this, so that there would be islands. For instance, the idea of a retreat. Just crossing the street doesn't make so much sense.

TM There's a "Why here?" aspect about it. Why would you build in such a landscape? In such an isolated way? It would almost suggest that it was some industrial process.

PB Well, it's also financed by Jordan and Israel. It's crossing a shared border, so that's one of the reasons, I suppose.

TM Right. Is it actually on the border?

CJ I just have a little bit of a difficulty with its manufacture, even these little symbols give it away. It has become an icon of plan and it's transplanted here. But, you know, in a landscape like this, you imagine that you have to have a very primary figure or gesture.

JP But, then, it would be a wall that encloses a paradise.

PB Then you—look what we see here. We see a kind of dried-up river area, which is very flat and has these marks and then enormous rock—that's enormous. They don't do anything with this. Isn't that strange?

TM Yes, there's no response to the landscape, really, is there?

CJ You know, it would be more interesting if the road—if one could accept this as a series of spokes. Extensions into the landscape or so, it would be more interesting that way. But the road is very peculiar.

JP I guess we have to move on.

DG What did you vote on **Bridging the Rift?**

JP We were not so keen on it, unless you want to keep it.

Jewish Medical New Inpatient Pavilion

Air Force Academy Cadet Chapel

CJ We had an interesting argument about it.

DG Okay, good. And this one is the **North Shore-Long Island Jewish Medical New Inpatient Pavilion.**

TM It's difficult to say anything critical about it, given that it seems like a natural addition to what was there and doesn't necessarily challenge what was there, looking at it. It was not a surprise and it's difficult to judge it in its context against the other buildings, because you can't really see what the other buildings are from a fabric point of view, but there's this suggestion that the glass façade and a colonnade should have something to respond to, but I'm not sure that's clear from here.

CJ And it looks quite pragmatic. I can't sense any special idea about the building.

TM Yes, I don't know whether—for a minute, I thought this pullout was a plug-in piece. You know, it was built of plug-in units, but I don't think it is really. It was just the description of what's in the room.

DG Right.

PB Well, I think it's totally in discrepancy with the description. It says that the new inpatient pavilion is the centerpiece of a revitalized campus. Well, I don't see it to be a centerpiece at all.

DG I don't know that it succeeds on any

of those grand claims that it makes for itself. But it is worth pointing out that this is one of the most difficult types of buildings to do because the medical requirements are truly daunting. And so even to produce it in a modest form but successfully accommodate all of these various needs in an awkward site, and to pull it together is already something reasonable.

PB And so each room is a particle of the façade. What also I read is that this whole center has a multitude of different specializations. It's both psychological—psychiatric institute—

DG And imaging and medical.

PB And so they need expansion for all the disciplines and then you build this kind of building or three or four disciplines altogether, then, with the expansion?

DG But maybe they are connected. Maybe they needed, for one reason or another, to put these groups together because it made sense. They don't usually put disparate things together in hospitals, particularly in a large complex like this, unless it makes sense. And so they must be seeing connections that perhaps we're not aware of.

I actually don't think it's a bad building at all. I don't think it's a great building, but I think it's—it's a modest building.

TM "Modest" is the right word, isn't it? Yes.

PB So do we keep it in?

DG Is it worth talking about more? Is there more that we would want to say about it? If we had it for another round?

TM I don't think it challenges enough for me to keep it in.

PB And I think then they maybe could have explained more why it is the way it is.

CJ Well, it's inherited this site plan that is a mess to begin with.

DG To have done anything and to not have made it worse is already an accomplishment. Okay, all right, move on, to the **Air Force Academy.**

PB This is such a beautiful building.

TM Walter Netsch.

PB From the '50s.

TM It was the first time that a designer was named from SOM as being responsible for a building; and he then went on to build the University of Chicago campus.

JP This is a very interesting problem which becomes increasingly typical when modern buildings need to be renovated. In that sense, it represents a problem that has not been studied very much anywhere so far.

400 Fifth Avenue

DG That's right. There are several projects that are renovations, restorations, adaptations. And so one might ask the question here, is this something that we would want to talk about a bit more?
TM Well, I could enjoy talking about it endlessly, actually.
PB Yes.
DG Okay, good.
TM Simply because it's dealing with what was a very fine piece of architecture to start with and which had a very complex construction program.

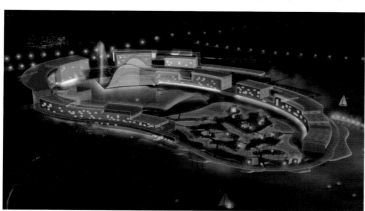

Bahrain Waterfront Master Plan

DG Let's come back to it, let's move ahead.
CJ This is an **Exhibit at the American Academy.**
PB Silence.
TM Did you see it there?
DG No, I arrived after it had been taken down.
CJ First of all, it's rather surprising to find such an almost minute project in the scale of all the projects we have seen. So there's something refreshing about the project on its own merit, but, I don't know, artistically, I'm curious what they intended to do to merge images. So I don't know if it is a naïve attempt to deal with art-making here.
PB Well, I don't think we should consider it as one of the five.
DG Yes, okay. And we don't really need to talk about it more?
CJ I'd much prefer to talk about ...
DG This is **400 Fifth Avenue.** I actually was interested in this, but I wanted your thoughts.
TM Well, I mean, I can declare an interest in that I have seen it before. And we have been asked to look at the wall, but from first seeing it, I enjoyed this whole process of trying to enliven the façade. It's a very simple idea. It's really just using precast cladding units, precast complete

cladding units to throw up a play.
DG The windows have to be on an angle.
TM Yes, they have to be.
PB And that's nice, too.
DG Yes. Okay, this is one that I think maybe we should come back and talk about, then.
CJ Actually, it's an accomplished project.
JP Is it presented just as a façade system, because there are no plans, for instance.
DG Let's come back to it. Let's move on to the **Bahrain Waterfront Master Plan.**
CJ God, Robert Smithson and—
PB Nature.
CJ Nature.
DG Is this a project that you want to talk about?
CJ I don't particularly.
TM No.
JP No.
DG It's actually tackling an interesting problem, but I don't know that it does it successfully.
PB Okay, so we could come back to it, if you want.
TM I kind of dismissed it because I've been along that waterfront which has the same sort of problem. And I just find it so difficult to feel enthusiastic or engaged with it.
DG It's a developer's project.
TM A developer's project, yes, there's no architectural impulse for it.
PB So it looks like tourism and Disney and developer combined.
JP It's more like a theme park, it has a theme park quality about it.
DG Okay, so moving right along.
PB ARB Bank.
CJ This is a powerful piece.
PB I like this one.
CJ Yes, I do, too.
TM Yes.
DG Okay, then let's come back to it, since we know we're going to talk about it later.
CJ Yes, it has something to say that is really wonderful.

DG All right, this is the **Schloss Velden** in Austria.

PB It wants to respect and keep the original castle as the center of this whole garden-park. So it doesn't want to disturb any of the attention for tradition.

DG I think this may be the only landscape project here.

PB That's why I thought it was interesting.

DG I think we should come back to it.

PB What do you think, Juhani?

JP Well, I would like to come back to it.

CJ There's some idea here which is worth discussing.

JP A quietness about it.

DG **Carlisle Pier** in Dublin.

PB Okay, so, Tim?

TM I dismiss it too quickly, you know, it's a bit Liebeskind. I'm probably not taking the time to look at it seriously.

DG Well, now, you guys were talking earlier about bold gestures. You just don't like bold, derivative gestures?

TM That's right, that's exactly right. I think a bold gesture, when it's really derivative without developing something, is more difficult to accept.

JP There's a big difference between a bold gesture and something that is just gimmicky and I think this is of the latter kind.

DG I actually don't think this is gimmicky. I think this is trying to talk in a language that some people seem to find interesting today and it's not doing it badly. Just because somebody else did it first doesn't mean that the first one is the good one and this is the weak one.
And I think that there is something to say here. When you stick something like this in the middle of Victorian London, it's something more than a bold gesture or perhaps less than a bold gesture. And this instead is an area that has traditionally been lost to the city. And so, it doesn't damage in the way that other sites might. I don't know that we need to come back and talk about this more, but I'm just not willing to dismiss it simply because it's derivative.

PB It's supposed to be "one of the powerful reminders of the achievements of Victorian engineers and entrepreneurs. A series of crystals, each crystal has a different function or a program. It contains museums, restaurants, retail facilities—" But it looks like a cruise ship.

DG We're not coming back to this, so, okay. **444 North Michigan Avenue**. And this is a lobby redesign, as I understand it.

CJ Yes, this is where they actually transform the lobby through color manipulations. Atmospheric color manipulations. That's pretty much all that happens, isn't it? Except for the texture on the floor and the wood.

PB I don't think it's worth keeping

DG Okay. **The Smithsonian Museum of American History**.

PB Now there you have something.

CJ I love the hard maple.

DG This is another restoration project.

CJ Well, it's recycling more than restoration. It's interesting, the way they want to evoke history by recycling every barn and every piece of glass.

TM Yes, and making the glass with glass bottles, that's a very odd thing to do. I mean, it would be a lot of energy to fabricate the glass bottles and it costs a fortune to make glass like that.

PB "... spatially unifying north-south spine experience, new entry pavilions, a new box for 'The Star-Spangled Banner' with a significant and choreographed entry experience and new galleries for the west ... "

DG Maybe the confusion is that the presentation isn't clear to us, exactly what it's doing and where, even though there's lots of drawings; somehow, there's a failure to help us understand exactly what's being connected.

CJ Well, that's the problem I have with the project. There is so much information in it

Carlisle Pier

and, yet, it cannot be connected. I couldn't figure out if it is new or old.

DG Well, they didn't use all the space that could have to make it clear to us. But there are some very smart things here—it's blocks of glass and I thought that was quite beautiful.

PB And they take out a piece of the new spine, a visible storage passage-way. That I found a very interesting idea, that you create a museum where storage is visible to the public. You can go into it, so the museum is like the library

Smithsonian Museum of American History

of objects. And that seems nice.

DG I think we should come back to it and look at it a bit more. This is the **Poly International Plaza.**

CJ It seems very dense, the structure. It's interesting, a very iconic building.

DG Right.

CJ We have other examples of more accomplished towers of this nature, I think.

DG The next one is the **Jinling Tower.**

PB It's too flimsy a structure and it talks about this is as like the Chinese tradition, that you have all kinds of arrival points leading to the central part and to the north plaza. So they're doing all these sequences.

DG Okay, this is **Chaoyang Plaza.** If you look at this particular drawing, it looks as if you have floating panels on the exterior, which could be extremely interesting. And then they did all of this complicated frit-work. They made the thing much more complicated and took away the elegance and purity of these lines here.

PB Do you know why? Because they want that someone can go through; all this is really beautiful. If you have the building section like this, all your floors would have landscape-like connections. And what they do is they just make a thread of the floor, so they don't lose the building quality.

DG Right. And they don't lose the elegance, the purity and simplicity of their first concept. They carve it out instead. I found this quite beautiful. I was really attracted to that. **The New Beijing Poly Plaza.**

PB Yes, it's beautiful ... it's kind of interesting.

DG Is this one of the ones that we're going to discuss at length?

CJ I think this—there is something worth discussing here.

DG Okay, well, then, let's put that in and go forward. **Pin-Fuse Joint™.** I confess, I love this.

This is in? Move forward. **Christ the Light Cathedral,** Oakland, California.

TM Santiago Calatrava. Do you know that?

CJ Yes.

PB I think this should go out.

CJ Yes.

TM Yes.

PB I think it's such useless layers of stuff.

CJ It's so overdone.

PB Totally decorative decisions and probably, there's about five times more office space and parking than there is cathedral.

DG I don't know about that. This is the Christ the Light Corporation.

CJ Corporation. Oh, this is a corporation.

DG This is a religious corporation. There's some possibility, but somehow, I don't believe that it's going to come through that.

TM It's Calatrava's design, first of all. And they didn't obviously build Calatrava's design.

CJ There is almost a gap between the invention and the reality.

DG Okay, so this is **Shanghai Yangpu University.**

PB The campus, and this is the historic site. Beautiful. And then they're going to fill up everything, a new middle with a campus full of buildings.

CJ There's something very puzzling on this campus. Mapping is like almost an apology, perhaps.

DG But that's one of the things that comes straight out of architecture school.

CJ You have to shed that, because that's

Poly International Plaza

Chaoyang Plaza

The New Beijing Poly Plaza

just a beginning. You can't remain with this.

DG But so much is taught this way. How do we get beyond that and how do you think beyond that?

CJ But I think the architecture reflects or is indicative of the confusion. And when you think about this connection here of the textures that are applied, the different divisions between the pieces of the building, even the odd way by which they come together, it's all so disjointed, you know? Because if you think "Yes, I can accept this as a texture and the inspiration of a texture," but where does it lead? Where does it go? Where did you find it?

PB So this refers to this?

CJ I imagine it's some kind of fabric or texture applied to the building, but it's not even clear.

JP It doesn't appeal to me, in any way.

DG I may be old-fashioned, but I think that a university ought to have something more poetic. And this is about the function. Pure, simple function. And even if they are thinking about different textures, there's nothing about how these things come together, how they relate to one another.

PB Yes, but also not to what's there. It really could be anywhere. There is no respect for what culture you've inherited. There is no refinement, it's just there.

TM Yes, you're all looking at the building, not looking at the views.

DG This is the one image, I thought that actually could have some promise.

CJ Yes, that one, because it clarifies the pieces.

DG But then it should have been subjected to the kind of rigor of that gateway.

PB Maybe the scale should be ten times smaller, I don't know.

CJ There's a lot one could speak about in this project, because there is, obviously, a sensibility of intention everywhere and, yet, it's missed in the architecture. The architecture seems foreign to that sensibility.

PB I think it's totally fake.

JP Yes, it needs to have some kind of a story.

DG Exactly. But let's be honest. This comes out of that first-year Bauhaus education and they never, ever get beyond it and I think in part because the faculty can't get beyond it. They themselves don't

know how to do these things.

CJ Diane is right. Habits.

DG Okay, where are we? The **Jiangbei City Center.** There are some things I liked about this.

PB It's just triangles with three faces like the sort of primitive, changing advertisement.

CJ So it's more like folding louvers.

PB Yes, they turn around and open and shut. And they also can be repainted or re-collaged when you want to change your image.

CJ Oh, I thought it was more like the library in Paris, where they actually used digital images projected from behind.

PB That's what we all thought, but if you see this, I don't think so. It's a fantastically beautiful park. And in that a 20,000-square-meter department store. 10,000 square meters, with a market, food, beverage, health. 10,000—office space, with a bank, management office, post office, building services and parking. This is a shopping center. In the middle of a park, so that's a revolutionary commission.

Shanghai Yangpu University

Jianbei City Center

Tysons Corner Development

Pritzker & Hyatt Corporation

DG Okay. **Transit Oriented Development Tysons Corner.** This is in Virginia. My problem with this one was that it said there were two interesting bridges, and I don't know if the bridges were existing, or if they were to be built. It's not clear. There is going to be a traffic extension from Washington D.C. to Dulles Airport so there will be more planes. It's highly technical to do this type of project. It's just that I don't exactly understand what they are doing there.

PB Here you can see what they are—existing residential is light yellow, existing commercial is light blue and what they implement is the darker tone. And the whole concept, apparently, of this whole very commercial site that already exists is the mixing of living and working.

DG And it's a master plan. But there's something about the connection from level to level that I don't see. I think that there's something—to me it's too schematic. So this one is out.

Moving along. **Pritzker & Hyatt Corporation.**

PB This looks interesting. I can see. It's quite intriguing, don't you think?

CJ That it is.

DG It's my understanding this is an existing skyscraper of which there is going to be these floors out across this and

turning it into a corporate headquarters.

JP Is it?

DG It's new headquarters, but is it integrated within the existing hotel?

PB Corporate headquarters, and then you get very special atmosphere here where people feel at home, like in a hotel room, yet—

CJ You're in the office.

DG If that's the case, then there's something profoundly confusing about the way this is presented because it shows no location. It shows no ground plan; it shows nothing about how this connects to the earth, period. And I thought it was giving a slice. I thought it was a slice of an existing building but it was then being transformed.

TM There's no hotel room, is there? That's just offices?

CJ Offices. Or they're combining them.

TM Can you sleep in your office?

CJ The shape seems to suggest some of actuality in some site, and yet we don't have a site plan.

JP There is a comparison plan here.

DG You see what can happen? This is an existing building, and I think that's it.

PB Yes, it looks like it.

TM I think this is showing you a slice of the building.

CJ It's just a dimension of the same section, but enlarged.

PB The project is a sequence of representational zones and workspaces through the use of unifying architectural expressions and materials. So one of the ways they do that is to create furniture and finishes of wood that leads to things like wooden tables, wooden benches.

JP It shows a lot of detail, but then the whole site plan, we don't even know how many floors we have.

PB It's a detail work.

CJ It is very, very oddly presented, absolutely. It's confusing.

TM What I really don't understand—look, here are our lifts. Impossible. That can't be true. So this is what we've started with. And then they create an atrium somewhere, whether it's the top of the building or whatever, because those lifts must have gone to the top at one time, right? And here they are right on the plan here.

DG Okay, I think we can move forward. But I think this is a project where certain aspects of the presentation are very interesting, but it's so confusing that we simply can't make a judgment. Next, **Columbia University Master Plan** in Manhattanville, New York.

TM This is being done at the Renzo Piano workshop. One thing that's something quite adventurous here is to create a whole underground level of services for this whole complex. It's a 30-year master plan, so it's happening piece by piece, but the concept seems to be to take the whole underground zone covering that whole site and using it for service, which must be a fairly rare thing. In turn, it enables it to have the access to do that in one part. So I think the bigger news is quite exciting.

JP Maybe if we understood what it is about.

DG Okay, I think that means we're going to move on. The next one is **St. Albans**.

PB It tells us about Olmsted Park and about the National Cathedral, but it doesn't really say what it does with them, except connecting—it's a bit naïve in a way.

CJ There's lots of study and research.

PB It's just a plane and metals, that's how I look at it.

CJ You can see here. They make it out of pieces.

PB Not unless their commission is to make a model.

DG They haven't designed it yet.

PB What I like about it—if I understand right—if you could do everything just with slight, slight things, then it's actually quite interesting.

DG And connectors.

PB And connectors literally very thin.

DG Let's leave St. Albans and come back to it. **Jebel Ali Lighthouse Marina**.

CJ I actually like this idea of the tent that is multi-folded and in sections it's more interesting.

DG It's the real world, though, so if you're going to do these towers—if you're going to accept that these towers are being done, and they are, then is this one that we want to look at more?

TM I actually quite like the gesture of the great folding plates.

DG And it's quite well handled. I think in this case it's actually well handled. It's controlled.

JP It's a little bit like the Yokohama Ferry Terminal.

TM Yes, looking at the structure and wondering how you would finally manage. Actually, it's a spoke technology, plate technology to make it, and in some sense it was quite conventional. One was kind of hoping that it would generate a slightly different approach to structure that would be more friendly towards this sort of plane-making, distortion-making move. It builds you into a set of problems, but as a gesture, I think it's quite interesting.

DG Do you want to talk about this now?

PB Yes, I think so, of course, I was jumping to chop it off, but on the other hand, the commission there is the Dubai

Columbia University Master Plan

Development Corporation. They probably want a landmark. It is the light tower, and what they do is they put program like hotels, restaurants, and offices in the tower, but personally, I would think that they should challenge their client more and say, "Why don't we put that program in the pier itself?" Have everything there and create a light tower that is only a light tower, a very thin needle.

CJ They're already doing that. They're distributing retail and entertainment.

PB We're talking six enormous aquariums, so it looks like a bit of a wasted space also down there.

DG So we're going to come back and talk about this.

Let's move ahead and see what else we've got. **The Canadian Museum for Human Rights.**

TM You have this diagram. We have these boxes and the thought was how do you connect them, and it was, oddly enough, sort of a Seattle-like response. You connect the top edge of that box with the top edge of that box, etc. But what I don't think they convincingly demonstrated on any of the drawings here is that the boxes truly stand up, particularly the main one facing us here. Being the engineer, I have to say that I would try to reinforce that and help to define vertical structure elements.

DG This is the **Skyscraper Museum** in New York City.

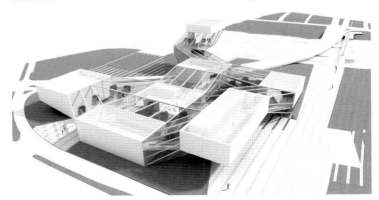

Canadian Museum for Human Rights

Dubai Sun Tower

CJ This is built?

PB It's built.

CJ It's a very small space.

DG And this is **Dubai Sun Tower**.

CJ It's worrisome when you have this kind of space.

DG Do you want to keep and talk about this? Anybody?

CJ I think we have better examples.

DG Okay. Now we move to the other room. **T2 Sky Plaza**, Hong Kong.

DG This is a skin and a covering problem, so do we want to keep this in and talk about it more?

PB It is an interesting subject at the moment—airport and transportation of huge amounts of people.

DG It's both ferry and airport.

CJ It's interesting, but really, you're only always seeing the treatment of the exterior and the roofscape.

DG I think that's what the problem is here.

PB Softening the surface of the box.

DG And I actually like that façade. The modeling of the surface. I like that movement. There's something almost Baroque about it.

PB It suggests movement. Because you

pass by, it opens up and it closes and so on. But is it an effect or is it also construction, Tim?

TM It's purely effect, for sure, and that's what's rather disappointing for me is that when I see it, it's a very applied thing.

DG This is a shed. So what do you do with the shed? If you don't want another Wal-Mart, what do you do? I think this is potentially elegant.

PB But does it make the roof stretch much without columns or does it do anything? Does it hold up the roof? Is it a stretch, pull, push, float, whatever situation? What is it? What does it do?

TM There are slits of roof lights here—skylights, but I can't quite get a section to demonstrate what happens clearly. Nor do I really understand what happens when you go inside the building, and there seems to be a complete focus on these external elements as the principal design ideas. But I can't actually see what happens. There are a couple of levels missing.

PB "The solution of a big gesture roof typical of most contemporary airport terminals was deemed inappropriate. It was considered both unnecessarily

expensive and in conflict with the distinctive roof profile of the existing terminal." Is it actually an existing box, though? "The solution instead focused on the exterior of the building. However, this proved to be the most challenging component of the design process."

DG Maybe this is purely the façade. But it says, "Terminal Two." It's an addition. Is it a new building?

TM I think it's a new building.

PB It looks as if it already exists. Anyway, it's only about the cladding and I don't think we should put anything in the five that only talks about cladding. Do you think so?

DG I'm not prepared to say yet that because cladding is a problem, since it is so much of what architects do now in these larger buildings. When it's beyond the scale of a house, it really is about cladding—these office buildings or these massive people containers, and so then to me it poses an interesting question. The real question here is whether this cladding is sufficiently interesting to make us want to keep talking about it?

CJ I agree with you about the cladding as an idea, but I worry about the elements that are suddenly very clumsily attached to the cladding like the terminal extensions, the way that it opens. It seems to me that the beauty of an object like this is to be that pure because it is that way. Look how it's shown here. It is an amazing membrane, but when I look at it more closely, you realize that they're very strange juxtapositions that defy that investigation of the pure envelope and the membrane. And that's what bothers me about it, personally.

DG Is that the seaside, the water ferry entrance, or is that a public transport entrance?

CJ In the plan it doesn't mention it.

DG Those are already problems, because if we knew what it was, we would be better able to assess it.

CJ But I do like this concept of alleviating and bringing a scale to the gigantic box. I think you're absolutely right. I just think that when you do such a gesture, more attention should be given to these critical pieces.

PB I think that's more work that people like me are supposed to do. It's not about an ingenious building. It's not about a fantastic layout, program, energy, construction. It's just about a layer that enriches the building.

DG That's what a lot of Renaissance architecture was about, though. Let's face it.

CJ They were doing it with great success, too?

DG In a lot of cases, it was one architect who did the façade and then somebody else thirty years later who did the interior or somebody thirty years earlier did the interior. Somebody else comes along and does the façade. You can go see many of them, and you'll see that revetment literally grafted on the front of a building, sticking up beyond the roof line. A classic example, which is part of an ensemble, is the Senate building at the Campidoglio in Rome.

TM So that you as observer from the street experience the architecture as a piece.

DG Of course. So I'm not saying that one should design in the same way today. What I'm saying is these buildings are buildings that you fly by on the freeway, or better yet, in the air, coming or going. What do you do to this skin to give it an arresting quality from various distances? It is skin.

JP What bothers me is that it is presented as a kind of façade instrument, but in fact it is just decoration. If these elements reacted to the sun or did something else functional. I would like them to do something else than being just a decoration.

DG So much for me will depend upon the materials that they use and the way these elements look at different times of day and with different conditions of light and how they age. So there are a few questions that I have unanswered. I see a lot of potential in this. Well, where are we on this? I've made my big arguments for this. Is it in or out?

PB I'm not persuaded. Tim, are you persuaded?

TM I have mixed feelings about it. I think I have to say no. I like what it's attempting to do, but I think it's wasteful. Why use all that material like that. It's a real shame, because surely they could have thought of something more economic that would have generated the same thing. It wasn't intelligent in the way it was made. It might have been intelligent in what it was trying to achieve or it may have thought it was. I didn't think it was.

I would hope that if I saw this, I would also have the surprise. It's a little bit like looking at something and then you're always surprised when you get to the materiality of the thing. You think, "Oh, god. They did that. Oh!"

PB I agree with you that's a very important part of architecture. I've seen roofs like that from the '50s that do fantastic acoustic effects, and then all of the sudden it's blown up to a whole airport.

T2 Sky Plaza

Creative and Performing Arts High School

DG A whole terminal. Okay. So **Kuwait Military Academy Master Plan**.

CJ I already said that in my view this is much better than the previous master plan, which we saw.

DG Different purpose entirely. This is a military academy and the other one was a research center.

CJ We commented that in the other one, the circular paths seem to be so unrelated to the intricacy of the various spaces and I think here there is something very rich in the tapestry of these various courtyards and open spaces, with the surrounding perimeter, and it was more a comparison of formal choices for planning gestures.

PB It's very, very intense so it's like taking

out one block and putting it in like that.

DG Is this in? We can talk about it more?

CJ I think so.

DG Paterson Public School 25.

TM Don't get it.

DG Interesting. You're not sure exactly what's being done here, are you?

TM No. I'm seeing an indoor tennis court with a glass bridge above it. Maybe I'm wrong.

PB So there's an existing school at each point? Yes? And this is a new addition?

DG And then these are the plans of how the addition links up with the existing buildings on number four.

PB Those two, and this is the imagined volume of the addition—these lines here.

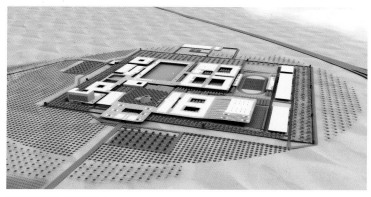

Kuwait Military Academy

TM Yes. That's it. And then this bridge is turned inner courtyard and some other inner thing going on.

DG See, this? It's connecting the two schools in the middle.

TM And another basketball pitch by the side. An indoor and an outdoor one. Well, I don't think it's particularly interesting. I don't know why we're looking at it all the time.

DG Well, we were trying to figure out what it was. So this is not in. Does this have a partisan?

PB I wouldn't say this is revolutionary.

DG Okay. Camden **Creative and Performing Arts High School.**

CJ I think it's interesting to see these two next to one another, because this one makes a far more interesting proposition, urbanistically, I think, and I like what it does to the area. That's a quite decimated urban piece, and the high school becomes this attractor for publicness. And I think it's done very well. And it even brings in this world of the teenager into the landscape of the interior.

DG This is one that we want to talk about some more, because I think I'm interested in this one. We have nineteen that stayed in. All right. Shall we start?

CJ The **Canadian Museum for Human Rights** has potential.

DG This is a case where, had the structural engineer or the consulting engineer been brought in sooner, this would have been most likely much more felicitously resolved. There would have been a dialogue to try to achieve the goals they were attempting to achieve these free-floating boxes.

PB And also I think if you read the text, the content of why they are boxes and what is in these boxes is unclear. They talk about five subjects on human rights, but they don't say what and they don't explain any philosophy behind it.

DG So this is out. This is the **400 Fifth**

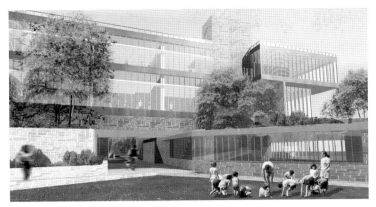

St. Albans School

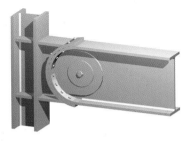

Pin-Fuse Joint™

Avenue. This is the façade ...

PB ... façade story.

CJ It's the same on every façade.

PB It's quite elegant in its size, but I think they have a nice play with it, but are they turning?

DG They don't turn. They turn on the model until they make the final decision. Actually, the thing that troubles me most is the atrium there—that opening looking over to the building across the street.

TM It's an enormous atrium space, in fact.

DG Let's keep this in for the moment—**400 Fifth Avenue,** and then we'll figure out how we'll proceed. This is **St. Albans.** Am I correct?

CJ I appreciate the initial gesture, but I don't know if there's enough substantiation for me to continue with it.

DG Yes, but one of the things that intrigued me about this project was that part of the task was to deal with something that hasn't been dealt with in the past. That is this 60-foot differential in height so one has to deal with ADA; how do people have access to different parts of the campus?

This isn't a grand skyscraper. This isn't grand architecture. This is taking something that was there, adding a few

things, but making it work in a way that brings it into the needs and demands that are as important in the 20th century. It's a really important task for architects to attend to; they've taken this seriously and they've attempted to bridge these different gaps in straightforward and modest ways that accomplish those goals. And that's already significant. And it does tie together the different parts of the campus.

PB That's why I like it, too. It's the first time I've seen this; and these tiny, little transparent boxes that create liaisons. It's the first time that they work with land-scape or modeling or topography and that's quite nice.

JP I would hope that there would be more suggestion of what it means architec-turally.

DG Part of why I'm attracted to this project is that it attempts to solve a problem. And we always hear that architecture is about solving problems. Usually the problem you solve is how to get as much money as possible out of a small site, how to make a building as tall as possible, how to deal with natural forces, and so forth. And this is a problem of how people can move through an already difficult site.

PB So the only thing they actually have is, I think, this little box here and this as

volumes? That's how I understand. Can't they be more clear?

DG So the problem is we're not clear on exactly what they're adding and seeing how they add it. We see the master plan, but we don't see how it actually fits together.

PB You see a bit here.

DG I would want to keep this in still.

TM There is quite a lot. Intervening can be quite a challenge.

DG All right, let's move on. The **Pin-Fuse Joint™.**

CJ It's something completely new.

TM It's tackling a problem which has been around for a while, and that's the problem of when an earthquake strikes a building, the building gets set into motion, and if it's got a motion which is approximately close to the impulse of the earthquake, then it will go into a resonance and fall apart. You know what's nice is that it all fits within really standard detailing. It's all within that effect. I think this is one of the simplest, cleverest applications of this type.

JP Does the structure return back to its original state?

TM Yes, it does, and that's the great thing, once the friction is overcome, it can return back to its original state without anything having to be remade in this joint.

China Energy Corporate Headquarters

DG Isn't that wonderful?

PB It's more like a clock.

DG So this is in. The **Pin-Fuse Joint™** is in still. And then here's the **Air Force Academy.**

PB That has to be explained also, because it's such a beautiful building that there is a concern with what you do to better it.

TM I share that concern, but I think what they're saying in the text that I read was that the renovations until now have actually caused further damage. Filling earth and sealants into the joints, these are inferior maintenance and the urethane fillers were discoloring the aluminum cladding.

DG So that instead of just putting an "umbrella" or a "Band-Aid," they want to put an "umbrella," a "raincoat," and "boots" on it. I loved that imagery.

CJ But he also talks about the idea of restoration for modern buildings. It brings to attention the fact that these are historical buildings of value and therefore they must be restored to their original status.

TM It's kind of a metaphor for what you'd like to see in SOM, which is a continuity in the integrity with which they consider something. When you look at this

construction, taken apart, I'm absolutely intrigued. I just want to get further into it because I know that everything looks like it's been thought through to a degree that it will interest me. If you look at this joint here, the articulation in that joint is quite extraordinary, just locally. And the panel here and the complexity of the unidirectional anchor. And look at those beautiful pieces there.

PB This is before and after. So this is what we all like, and it's fantastic, but now what are they adding? This is a very important detail. What's been done between 1960 and 2003 they're now taking out. That's a good move. But then what are they going to do?

DG There's a series of things that don't change. Here are these elements, but they've had these elements added to it. It looks the same in the end. This is such a clear presentation, and though I'm not that technically inclined, I did understand it. This is a very clear, coherent presentation. It pulls apart. It tells you exactly what's happened. We don't have to ask questions. They tell you what they take out, they tell you what the problems were. You get rid of the gutter, you get rid of the silicone and all these other things, and now we put in contemporary high

technology that ends up looking the same but acts better. They make this very clear in their drawings, so I'm very impressed with the presentation and the clarity of something quite complex.

JP The Alvar Aalto Academy which functions in this very building has organized two courses on restoration of modern buildings. It is becoming a very big problem in Europe and presents completely different and more severe problems than restoration of old buildings, simply because there are such untested inventions which were used in the modern period.

DG It's a little bit like the frescos and mural paintings that were done in the '30s that are in worse condition than murals that were done 500 years ago, because those technologies were time-tested already, and in the modern period, they tried all these new materials and so forth, and they decay and they deteriorate quite rapidly. And so this was the high technology of the time, but it has incredible limitation.

PB So that's staying in.

DG I say this stays in.

JP I would keep it also.

CJ Yes, I would also.

DG Okay, the next one is **China Energy Corporate Headquarters.**

JP I think we kept it because we didn't quite understand it. Do we now?

CJ This is a premise that is similar to the one that Mr. Gehry did in Berlin, where there is a very rigid framework upon which is inserted this more bucolic and bimorphic shape. It's almost a replica.

JP This says a "structural optimization diagram." What does it mean?

TM Your guess is as good as mine.

PB They say that this project attempts to respond to energy in several ways. Movement to the side and within the building is expressed in the form of the landscape in the lobby. The façade reveals the flow of energy in the building structure. New technologies for the conservation and generation of energy have been incorporated into the building and landscape so that they can be seen in action.

DG The concept here is that this is going to be constantly changing—I like that.

CJ So that it communicates the energy changes.

DG But I thought that there was something about the energy uses here that there was some element that was going to convey different types of energy uses at different times of day or year or light conditions.

TM There does seem to be this organic chimney-like object inside here.

PB A large exhibition hall to demonstrate energy technology. The side of the building has been designed to show the pattern of the flow of energy in the structure.

DG Yes, that's what makes this interesting. These forms and then the way they act and become a demonstration of what the building is about. I think that's a very interesting idea. And it makes it far more interesting than Gehry's, which is just about sculpture and wood. This is alive. This is vibrating. This is pulsing.

PB If it's not a live thing that changes, that makes visible what's really happening, then it's, of course, kitsch again, because then it's a decoration.

DG So we must believe that they say what they're doing.

PB But they symbolize it in the landscape, because obviously here it doesn't happen, but they sort of symbolize energy and flow.

CJ But how do we feel about these buildings that use this initial gadgetry that eventually falls apart?

DG If you're going to say that then we wouldn't have done the **Air Force Academy** because it depended upon all sorts of gadgetry to make this stuff, all this glass.

CJ That's a more static condition, isn't it?

JP Jean Nouvel and all his cameras shutters, which do not seem to function anymore.

DG Well, that doesn't work, but I'm prepared to accept that maybe this does. This is the central electricity building, and what it's supposed to be doing is explaining or demonstrating or evoking those energies.

PB But we're not completely convinced.

JP I think it's more verbal camouflage than anything else.

CJ It's primarily a graphic exercise in many ways. Because when you start to really analyze the flow of these drawings, the graphics are beautiful, but the eventuality of the building—I don't know if it will result in this. That's my doubt.

JP Is this a competition entry or is there some reality behind it?

PB It's a competition. It says here, "Competition 1.5 million-square-foot Beijing office building."

DG In or out? How many votes?

PB I think it's out.

DG Okay, the **Columbia University Master Plan** for Manhattanville.

TM This doesn't give, in any great sense, an idea of what that place would be like. You want to have some faith in this. It

wouldn't be the balancing influence of another architect who's obviously someone of international recognition and renown. Hopefully together they could create something extraordinary. But what I found amazing about the whole six blocks—a major slice of Manhattan. It's four blocks in between two fairly wide avenues, and they've actually taken the whole underground space as a common linking vault.

CJ They take the areas beneath the highway.

TM Well, the streets go through here. You continue the grid. It's a big gesture.

PB And the technology is going to be there, or is it for people to be in?

TM I think it's mainly technology. If you look at that diagram, we see a little glimpse of what it might be. So I think it's the master plan exercise. It's dealing with two things: how do you integrate these buildings into being part of a university campus and at the same time keep the university's property pattern porous, so you've still got all the streets engaging and running through.

PB But what about the buildings themselves?

JP This is a rare example in America of an attempt to collect rather than disperse.

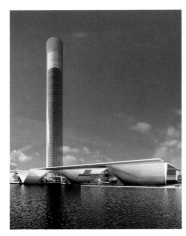

Jebel Ali Lighthouse Marina

West Bay Office Tower

ABC Street Studios

CJ I also like the way that this is existing infrastructure that is then part of the urban fabric. That's the great part.

DG I know, we'll come back to it. Let's do this, the **Jebel Ali Lighthouse Marina.**

JP This is a bit Disneyland, this folded plane, a little like a student project, when you begin to think realistically what would happen in this gigantic apartment, they wouldn't be near to what has been presented.

PB It doesn't take its potential from that.

DG This I voted to keep in. I still want to talk more about this.

DG And then we had this: the **West Bay Office Tower.**

TM I know we had a slightly deeper discussion about what the structure was doing here, and as Petra quite rightly pointed out, what's happening with the external columns is that they're reducing in dimension as they proceed upwards, so you do have in this diagram here a larger, bigger column than you do up here, so you're getting a breakdown.

PB You see it here. This is low and this is high, so it becomes thinner and thinner, and that is quite interesting, I find. Because it's so much thicker here you can be much more open.

DG OK, next is **ABC Street Studios,** I wanted this one. I just like the treatment of this elevation, giving it life and dynamism. You weren't persuaded by the **China Energy Company,** so I'm not sure you're going to be persuaded by this one.

TM That's odd because Chicago is like Athens as New York is like Rome. All the buildings there are sort of four-sided—a lot of them in Chicago. And this is a façade element, and that's just sort of a rare thing. It's just something stuck-on, as you were saying about Renaissance buildings being stuck-on. This is a contemporary stuck-on and I like it for it's bizarreness from that point of view. It's a very un-Chicago thing.

CJ It also harkens back to the previous life of this street where this illumination of façades was part of the activity of the city.

TM That's interesting.

CJ There's a certain nostalgia about the project.

JP Does it explain the technique of these images?

PB It's a media screen?

CJ It's a media screen. It could be anything. It's a projection.

JP It doesn't mean much, a "media screen."

PB Media screen, horizontal bracing and it looks like it penetrates the old building, so it anchors into the building with a definite space.

DG ABC is one of the big television media network conglomerates, so to have something like this is actually quite appropriate for the client. It really does talk about media, ephemerality, light, communication. I actually think it's quite clever.

TM I think it's fun. New York has a lot of things on buildings that do this—big advertising, but Chicago doesn't really have any of it. Chicago's a bit more poor-faced in that way.

PB This is much more ethereal.

CJ I like the way they disappear like a void.

DG I'm interested in leaving this one in.

PB Is there anything on this one?

DG So we didn't do this one yet, **ARB Bank,** so in or out?

CJ I like it, too, actually. It's one of the most inventive schemes that we have seen, I think. I like the force that it has in this desert landscape. It's quite powerful, and the idea that it's also an internal space—the way that it's all about internal illumination and protection of that interior world.

TM And even to the way the light comes through the wall.

JP It's very inventive.

TM That's a little bit like in Ronchamp where you never see the source of the light.

CJ But you notice in the section it's a series of courtyards and venting mechanisms—the light and the air.

TM The big problem I always had with buildings being built in the Middle East was that they were always replicas or symbols of Western architecture and culture and wealth, whereas this is somehow different—I love this image of the ground cracking and the light emerging.

PB It's just a beautiful building. It also organizes views, which I think is interesting, they're thinking about what you will see.

CJ It is very intelligent in the way that they can do a sustainable structure without all of the paraphernalia of sustainability that is becoming so obnoxious of late. Suddenly they're just saying, it's noise, shade, wind, dust, and blast.

PB It's really well explained also.

CJ It's so clear.

JP It is rammed earth.

CJ There's the same up here, a very solid exterior to protect the interior world, and the delicacy of the line.

PB I'll read it because it's really nice. "ARB Farmer's Bank is conceived as a series of earth forms within an active farmland that will change with seasons." That's also beautiful. Cultivation around it is imagined as part of the building.

DG I don't think we have any question. This one's in.

CJ Very intelligent.

PB The centerpiece of the project is a cistern.

DG What I think we would like to do, what I'd like to do now is go through and vote.

PB But we didn't discuss that yet. Is that still in?

JP Schloss Velden, the landscape piece?

TM We wanted it in.

DG I think we agreed that we were going to have it in. We've talked about all the other ones that are still in. We should talk about the landscape one, too. It is a beautiful project.

PB The spa is a new piece of landscape rising from the edge of the lake. It takes advantage of its unique location adjacent to the naturally linked pools of the Schloss site. This is a theme that has been carried into the spa. This is in the southernmost province of Austria. If I may have one critical note, it is that the story is more beautiful than the reality in the sense that I think they are really buildings. If you look here, it's hidden behind the trees, but they really exist. Look here, for instance. You can't say that it's a hardly visible fold.

CJ It appears and disappears.

TM I think one of the other problems I have with it, and this is just a visual impression, is the shape that some of the spaces become. They don't feel comfortable.

CJ I don't mind them in these rooms; in the rooms themselves they're more mathematical in precision. They multiply.

TM But I feel rather ill when I see that shape of room.

JP Even the bed tends to become trapezoidal.

PB But isn't that interesting that each room has a different plan? It's the first project of SOM I see in the whole series where they really think about the floor plan, in the sense that they are creative with it. That each time you have a new room, you come again and you have a totally different experience.

TM At a three-dimensional level, I think these three-dimensional images are great. I really enjoy them.

ARB Bank

Schloss Velden

Skyscraper Museum

PB So that's what you get. Each time you come in, you think, "Hey, something's happening."

CJ Yes, these are very compelling. They suggest that the new hotel extension is really a series of lifted terraces.

PB It's beautiful and it's simple.

DG It's seductively simple because it's not really that simple. It's actually incredibly complex.

CJ Of course, to find your room here is going to become an adventure, this landscape of purity is going to be interrupted by all kinds of signage.

DG This is the **Skyscraper Museum.** It's in Battery Park. It's one and a half stories.

PB It's an existing building? It shows endless heights and lows and so on, because of the mirroring.

DG Yes. And then these are printed on the glass, these images of famous skyscrapers. So for a small, elegant little project, this is quite wonderful.

OK, moving on, there are six top vote getters. They are the **West Bay Office Tower**; **ARB Bank**; the **Pin-Fuse Joint™** got three. The **Air Force**

Academy got four. And the **Schloss** had four votes. **Camden Creative Arts Academy** had three votes. Now we're down to six. Looking at this group, what do you all think?

CJ I like this scale.

TM These two show the most distinctive sense that they're pursuing a particular direction.

DG Which two? You need to say it.

TM The **ARB Bank** and **Schloss.**

PB And I think, restoration and the structure are things that I would really love SOM to continue doing because they traditionally have been inventors in those directions.

TM Yes. That's the symbolism, isn't it? They're both metaphors.

PB They're stimulating.

TM They're stimulating because everyone loves SOM historically. There is just this great respect for what the firm has done. Everyone wants to see the firm continue to blossom into doing the same thing again.

PB Or the same quality. Not the same thing.

TM Not the same thing; I mean the same

quality, of course, and I agree also that behind the architecture of that period, one always got the sense that there was a strong technical imagination. That's why I like this little pin idea. I think it should symbolize faith in that, and I think there's been a lot of environmental stuff discussed, but at times it seems to drive almost a fashionable response to the façade or the architecture. And I think the Bank is seriously taking on board what you do when you build in the desert, from an environmental point of view.

CJ What's extraordinary to me about the bank is that it's the first project that I felt completely convinced that they had really looked at where they were building.

PB Where and why.

CJ The way that they start first with the notion of cultivation, cistern, water, monolith, labyrinth. These amazing themes that are present in this part of the world, and they don't really trivialize them. They make an iconic piece. In some of the other projects we saw the trivialization of this imagery, and I think here the memory of these already iconic elements, they are so strong. And they become for me almost like the power of the imagination to invent something totally unique and at the same time recall back what these monolithic pieces were in the desert. And that is astonishing to me. That's one of the strengths of SOM. It was always about this kind of invention of something that seemed rather obvious. And I think the landscape piece is suggestive, too, because it starts to promote a direction of sculpting with the ground and merging that ground into an existing structure and inventing in the process. And I think in that sense it ties also back to the chapel which basically uses this incredible image of the wings and turns them into a sacred space. It's very powerful.

PB If I may do a critical note to the landscape. I think we also all subconsciously chose it because it is such an original thing for them to do—landscape. If you look at it critically, it's a very luxurious commission in a completely unpolitical, unstrenuous, un-urban, uneconomic, completely dreamy circumstance. And so it's quite easy to make something good out of it.

DG And they did.

PB And they did. So it's interesting because it's SOM and because it is half-buried and artistic in a different way, but I don't think it's intellectually or contextually the most incredible project or anything. It's more a choice to symbolize a direction that we'd like them to maybe also discover.

DG But it's also taking seriously that there are luxury markets. This is a spa for a luxury market, so how can you do this so it doesn't become a festering sore on an otherwise quite beautiful landscape? And I think they've done it quite well, actually. You mentioned earlier, Carlos, that you really like the range of scales, and I think that without even thinking about it or without planning, we ended up going from the smallest joint to the skyscraper with virtually every range in between. If you consider the last group of projects that we have—the nineteen and then the twelve or the thirteen, and then bringing it down to these six. First of all, they explain what they're doing very clearly. The clarity of the presentation is suggestive of the clarity of the thought behind the project. There's nothing missing; there's nothing unclear. That presentation tells you something about the quality and the character of the project that's already there. And it's evinced in the project, and I think it's as true of the skyscraper tower as it is of the **Pin-Fuse Joint™**.

CJ Yes, I think the clarity and the legibility of the boards is evident, absolutely, and I think one of the most striking images for me is here in the **Pin-Fuse™**, just the association to this other, immediate, recognizable bone condition—this cartilage and tendon. It immediately says everything.

JP One observation which pleases me is that there is not a single typical corporate project, except perhaps the skyscraper, but even that project represents a fairly soft corporate architecture. By the way, that's the one that interests me least. But I believe the message is that even a big office today needs to move away from the corporate image towards a more humble and humane attitude, which all of the projects we have selected represent nicely.

CJ I think the **Camden** school is really an exercise in what you're saying, because at least personally what I found intriguing about the project is the attention to a context that doesn't come from anything more than investigation of that locale. We saw how this gigantic office of SOM travels the world over and brings a certain luggage with them. They cannot escape it. They are, after all, a major force of architectural production. But I think here what is very touching to me and very moving is the fact that they have spent an enormous amount of time and research in an area already decimated by urban forces outside of their control, and they find a new space. They find a new life in the city, and I like the way it's presented, too, where you have this black and white world immediately ignited into life by this investigation.

PB What is interesting also is that maybe none of us really thinks that the high-rise buildings of SOM are convincing enough.

That could be an interesting statement. Because the only reason we chose this one is because the tower is also a structural invention somehow or it has an intelligence in the way structure is used. Because the site is sort of in the middle of nowhere. It has no surrounding. It's like a lonely landmark.

DG But the fact is there are commissions like that. There are such buildings and they go up around the world. I think we said to ourselves when we went through that this one convinced us the most, both for the treatment of the ground and for this rather unusual treatment of the frame extending up and tapering at the top, which is a classic structural invention from the past, but it is rendered here in a very different way, and that's quite inventive.

PB Should we leave it in or could it be a statement to have no high-rise building at all in our selection?

CJ I think we should keep it; what's so striking about this building is its structural integrity. We saw many skyscrapers become a series of collages of their own moments, like the one in Tokyo, that was trying to be every façade available to the skyscraper, and with very curious pedigrees. When I say "integrity" and "honesty" about the piece, it is what they are. This is a tall tower and they can become rather beautiful in the landscape.

DG Within that landscape, they become the features. They become another landscape.

CJ The vertical landscape and horizontal landscape or treescapes. Also think about the section, too. This building is not skin deep. It's actually very layered. It has several layers. So environmentally, it's probably very intriguing, even though they don't give you much evidence of that, but I'm sure it is.

PB Well, I just like the fact that it's lifted so that the structure is also its feet, and that you have a world underneath.

CJ But another interesting issue is that

SOM is also an office about refining certain things. They refine certain concerns that have been critical for their development, and the skyscraper is one of their contributions.

DG Will you all be comfortable if these six projects are the final choices, or is there something that you feel should go out?

CJ I feel comfortable with everything.

JP Yes, I do.

PB Yes, also.

CJ I like this scale variation, not so much in terms of size but in terms of intentions.

DG The other thing is the clarity of presentation. I was so gratified to be able to see a project that you could grasp. These aren't simple, but you could follow them. You understood the concepts, where they were intervening, and you could follow through. If you paid attention, you understood everything. You didn't end up with questions, and I think that's important. All of these projects gave us enough to understand what was going on.

CJ One thing I wanted just to say for the benefit of the restoration one is I learn a lot through this project, actually, about the nature of forty-five years of technological advancement. What you find is that they found the value in this project to restore it. That's very encouraging for a modern building.

DG And so that lack of care in the original project in the **Air Force Academy** is what bothers me the most, and when I see that same lack of care in contemporary projects, I'm bothered by it. So I'm happy that they're going back and discovering ways to deal with that.

CJ It's a pedagogical exercise for me, because it will teach an office of this magnitude that the experimentation has to be countered with a great deal of certainty and research, and I think today modern architecture is so suspect because it's more inventively ahead-of-its-time. It's no longer capable of sustaining its own predictability. We love buildings

because they appear so quickly today, but we know that they have a very short life.

JP And not only technically. An even more fundamental problem is that architectural aesthetics have become detached from the realities of construction. In the old days, the aesthetics was the roof and gutter and all the other elements which are needed for the building to be sustainable. Whereas in the days of modernity and even today, we tend to eliminate all that because our aesthetic aspirations are about something other than the realities of construction. The real essence of architectural beauty should really be taught again to students. That is where the true aesthetic qualities lie, in acknowledging the realities of construction, time, use, and wear.

PB I'm afraid that we also have to educate the clients then. Because I think the whole way that clients treat architecture doesn't really permit so much. Clients are also not aware of what the qualities could be and what the budget then also should cover.

JP The clients, builders and investors also tend to think in too short terms. They're only thinking of the costs at the moment of construction, not of the long-term ownership and use.

PB And effect—cost and effect. A very quick effect. It doesn't matter about the future.

DG The mere fact they designed the **Pin-Fuse Joint™**, to me, is a wonderful example of the kind of research that can and should take place in architectural offices for all sorts of problems.

CJ And for the restoration, it's more the fact that it is a self-critique. There is a very striking thing for me to see an office doing that and volunteering that.

PB Yes, but also the client allows the office to do it, because many clients don't even ask the architect to come back to do renovation work.

TM Everyone asks, "Why isn't

architecture at the same level as engineering and product development?" Well, you make one car and you invest fifty people all thinking about that one problem and they produce 10,000 of them.

PB But why do you make a division between architecture and engineering?

TM I make a division because I think engineering is actually a nomadic practice. I think engineers are nomadic and I think the whole instinct of the engineer is to go from A to B. The instinct is very different. Architecture's a kind of enveloping, encompassing, culturally enriching experience. The engineer is not involved with that. He's involved with this incredible sense of problem-solving. They can focus extraordinarily well on singular problems and come to very singular answers.

PB But in combination with the architectural story?

TM Well, in combination, it gets filled in. Today, we were talking about where can you find a good structural engineer who can have a conversation and be sympathetic? And all that's about, really, is that architects, in the end of the 19th century, suddenly realized that buildings were going to be built with steel frames and concrete frames. They were out there and they were being built by industry. They were all patented. But you couldn't interact with it closely, right?

CJ Yes.

TM Now, the only way you could interact with it closely is to bring an engineer into your team, a consulting engineer, someone who would actually say, "Hey, it isn't a concrete frame you want or a steel frame; in fact, it's a timber frame." And, then, they could say, "You don't need it to be just like that manufacturer saying it has to be. You can actually have this extraordinary, just-what-you-want thing." And that interaction, that design reliance between professionals really needs to

happen at a close level for this whole thing to move forward at a reasonable pace.

PB It's not about dividing them, because they need each other desperately.

CJ They need to be more integrated, absolutely.

TM They do, but the pure engineering does have a different discipline and a different direction, but engineering within architecture and actually used within architecture is different. The responsibility and the extraordinary thing is the whole industry sees this problem of the building falling apart. The whole failure, to some degree, of a lot of the architecture—the client's perception of the failure of architecture to deliver what they wanted has led to this curious trust in the contractor to deliver a building. I think the distinction between buildings designed by builders and buildings designed by architects, is profound. Buildings designed by builders are repeatable factory sheds, tract housing, whatever sort of repeatable unit that you get. Of course, the builder should go in and do it, but they don't need an architect to reconsider the thing ever and endlessly again. But every time you build a piece of architecture, it's such an integrated, articulated, specific thing.

CJ It's so unique.

PB I think the whole issue of restoration will be more and more important to take seriously and I think it's really luxurious, I find, in all senses, that the architects' group themselves can treat their own classic buildings. Which I think is a good mentality.

JP I don't believe that in Western contemporary architecture, we have at all seriously thought about longtime maintenance of buildings, in the sense that in the Japanese traditional buildings, for instance, components that have to be maintained can be taken apart. The necessity of renewal is part of the

architectural concept, whereas, this kind of thinking rarely occurs in modern buildings. Even in normal buildings in Japan, the components which are subject to rain can be taken apart without breaking the entire structure.

DG Does anybody else have any concluding remarks to make generally about our process today and our jury?

PB I was really very shocked. I was shocked when I saw the whole collection, because I had the feeling that an enormous office like SOM that inhabits many cultures, that works in many cultures, that they don't do much more sensitive, deep-going, less lazy research and depth or time in these projects to differentiate between Arab cultures, Asian cultures, Western cultures where they build enormous things and where they have—I mean, in China, they built twenty or thirty things. In the Arab world, ten towers, all of them landmarks, huge and capitalist to its peak. But they all look alike and they all have a shallowness to them, a real shallowness that I find is really making me angry and, respecting them in the past, even more angry. But I think why don't the people who lead this company stimulate their staff to do much more work and maybe then you don't gain so much money? Maybe you become poor, but at least you do the work.

JP That's a very difficult issue, even if the bosses and clients agreed to this task of cultural specificity in architecture. The question is can anyone build authentically within another culture? I doubt it, because culture is not a collection of motives or a collection of this and that. And, in many ways, culture cannot be learned, it has to be lived.

PB Yes, that's true.

JP And so I question the entire current practice that the same architects are building around the world. I think that's a very questionable thing.

PB That's a good point, yes.

CJ I'm glad you brought this up, because the reason I find this project **[ARB Bank]** so convincing is that it goes to something beyond the image of that culture. It goes to the root of the culture. This is a contemporary building, but enriched by this incredible knowledge of how it could function in this place.

PB And it's still a Western building.

CJ And then we saw these other examples of buildings that are as if they collect the greatest hits of the locality. And they say, "Well, this pagoda element, this other thing here," and it's very disrespectful and, in my view, trivializes the more important aspects of culture, which

educators take students to Europe or to China or to Africa, and we introduce them to a new culture, and then we ask them to design a project in three and a half months, in one semester, as if they could possibly imagine what this culture was like. So what happens? The classic example is everybody went to Italy and everybody came back to the States, generations of architects, wanting to design an Italian piazza, and nobody understood that they don't work because the culture and the people in the United States do not interact with their places the same way that they do in Italy. They think, "Oh, you put this in and

But you can combine that also with a kind of refinement for the context.

CJ The key is a sensitivity to a place. I think it still is the critical discourse, for me, in any architecture that we speak of. Even this project of the landscape **[Schloss Velden]**. There is a sensitivity about not totally destroying those views. And that is the true global currency today. It is this exchange of sensitivities that are cultural in nature and I think we negotiate with them, but we also impose them. And when we impose them, we create the anomalies that we have all over the world. Projects like this **[ARB Bank]** always give me a certain enthusiasm and a

Creative and Performing Arts High School

Schloss Velden

Pin-Fuse Joint ™

are really enriching to any building. China can have as many skyscrapers as it wants, but there must be something there that, with more time—and it's about time. And they don't have time. China is pushing with velocity here. They want progress, immediate progress.

DG Chinese architects know things about their culture that we don't. In virtually every project set in China, there was a courtyard with greenery in it, and that seems to be something that's a constant. And I don't know whether that trivializes the culture, because I really don't know it well enough.

This goes back to education. We as

people come. You have this and people come." They don't understand what it is about culture and history that makes these things alive and vibrant in one place and dead in another.

PB Well, there are two stories parallel, so maybe what I said wasn't very intelligent, in a way. Of course, we don't want that SOM or whoever builds according to culture in each culture that they are. Either SOM has such a strong backbone and philosophy and mentality that they have their very own language that can be refined, intelligent, it's about construction, it's about growth, future, whatever. And then it's recognizable wherever they build.

sense of optimism about what architecture can do, which is to better a place. That's its true currency. We cannot reproduce architecture like we can cars. We're not that fortunate, because it's a unique automobile in a unique set of conditions.

PB Yes, but we are a bunch of romantics in this jury. We're all really romantic, because we really pulled hard to put a lot of our imagination in what is being presented here. If I'm really being tough, I'm shocked by the superficiality of it and that everything is a mannerism on the surface, being very corporate and enormously flamboyant. But if you look at it one second, there is nothing behind it. And, together, we are sort of idealistically choosing these six—for instance, the school is also an ideological choice of ours, because we think it's a social build-ing, a community building, and it's inlaid in an urban condition. It helps people, it makes people happy. But I'm not sure that SOM itself brings that across.

CJ I think our role as critics is to extract the positive qualities in these projects, but also in presentations that are eliciting, in my view, not just seduction but critical thinking. I personally feel very good about the examples we have here, and we have kept them precisely

DG We also had some other ones, we did have to pare them down. I agree with you that I thought that there were lots of problem projects. Some in which I thought there were ideas but they weren't presented clearly, not enough information was given, not enough clear information. But there were others—the **ABC Street Studios**—I thought that was wonderfully inventive. It wasn't trying to be anything other than it was. It had a kind of transparency and clarity and link with the client.

A project such as that is about our contemporary world, and if we refuse to take on projects like that or refuse to

I did, too. Not enough to make it one of the final ones, but I think that we liked that quite a bit. We also liked the **Kuwait Military Academy**. I liked the **Bridging the Rift** project, the one in Jordan, although I thought it had some weaknesses.

TM I don't know whether architecture always has to have a person associated with it. When we speak about those days that SOM was producing all this wonderful work, we do actually associate the design with particular individuals. We do hear who they were and, in fact, a lot of them went on to develop their own work outside of SOM individually. There's a seed within

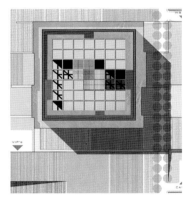

ARB Bank

Air Force Academy

West Bay Office Tower

because of that, because we detect a critical thinking about a place, about a program, about a condition.

And I couldn't agree with you more. Many of the projects we saw, I was completely turned off by the almost insulting persuasiveness of the seduction, which is a tool that we know doesn't exist, the landscape is not like that. And I agree totally.

But I also think that these presentations and these works really exhibit for me a very positive critical thinking in the office. And I think that's why I hope we can communicate to them that this is their future as well.

recognize them, then we do it at our peril. It is what Peter Rowe describes also is that middle landscape where we often interact with the rest of the world. And I think that actually makes that street and that building and that place better, that particular project.

PB So, should we put it back?

DG No, we already have six, so we can't put it back. But what I want to say is that there were many projects that had problems, but there were others that we might have kept, because some of us quite liked certain others a lot.

Tim, you quite liked, for example, the **Columbia University Master Plan** and

there that had the impulse and room to grow. I don't know why that is or why it was, it's there now and, if it is there, who is it that's emerging?

We're picking a group of schemes here that we think have potential and interest. And I wonder if the people we've chosen are recognized anyway within the firm as being people who are talented, who might be encouraged.

Jury Biographies

Diane Ghirardo

Diane Ghirardo teaches history and theory of architecture at the University of Southern California, Los Angeles, California, and the University of Cape Town, South Africa. She received an M.A. and Ph.D from Stanford University, was awarded two Fulbright Fellowships, is a Fellow of the American Academy in Rome, and a John Simon Guggenheim Fellow (2002–03). She has served as president of the Association of Collegiate Schools of Architecture (1993–96), executive editor of the Journal of Architectural Education (1988–99), and currently serves on the Board of Directors of the National Architectural Accreditation Board. She has published more than one hundred articles, book chapters, and criticism in publications such as Journal of the Society of Architectural Historians, Art Bulletin, Journal of Contemporary History, Lotus, Cite, Harvard Design Magazine, Perspecta, and Casabella. Among her translations of articles and books from Italian is Aldo Rossi's Architecture of the City. She has published four books: *Building New Communities: New Deal America and Fascist Italy* (1989, translated into Italian as *Le citta nuove nell'Italia Fascista e nell'America del New Deal* in 2003); *Out of Site: A Social Criticism of Architecture* (1991); *Mark Mack* (1994); *Architecture after Modernism* (1996), which received the Phi Kappa Phi award for excellence in 1997 and has been translated into French and Portuguese. In 1999, she was selected ACSA Distinguished Professor for outstanding Creative Achievement. She is currently researching and writing a book about women and spaces in Renaissance Italy, and a second book on the cultural history of architecture in twentieth-century Italy.

Petra Blaisse

Dutch designer Petra Blaisse works in architecture, landscape, exhibition, and textile design. In 1991 she founded Inside Outside, which specializes in the combination of both interior and exterior design, interweaving architecture and landscape. She has worked with OMA for the Netherlands Dance Theater, the Kunsthhalle in Rotterdam, the Grand Palais in Lille, Seattle Central Library, the Prada Stores in New York and Los Angeles, the Dutch Embassy in Berlin, and the IIT Student Center in Chicago. Her landscape projects include the Museumpark in Rotterdam, "Connective Landscape" in Seoul, Utrecht State Prison gardens, and Downsview Park in Toronto. Current projects include the Giardini di Porta Nuova in Milan and collaborations with Kazuyo Sejima and Ryue Nishizawa for the Glass Pavilion at the Toledo Museum of Art; with Toyo Ito for a hotel in Groningen, Holland; and with OMA for CCTV and TVCC in Beijing; and the Casa da Música in Porto, Portugal. Blaisse has exhibited her work at the Storefront for Art and Architecture in New York, Deutsches Architektur Museum in Frankfurt, and MOCA in Los Angeles. She has taught at the Berlage Institute in Rotterdam, the Academy for Fine Arts in Rotterdam, the Architectural Institute in Ghent, and UCLA, and has lectured at Harvard University, Technical University Delft, Cornell University, Academie voor Bouwkunst in Amsterdam, Netherlands Architecture Institute (NAI) in Rotterdam, UCLA, the Architecture League in New York, University of Texas School of Architecture in Austin, and the Illinois Institute of Technology in Chicago.

Tim Macfarlane

Tim Macfarlane founded Dewhurst Macfarlane and Partners with Laurence Dewhurst in 1985 and is the Creative Design Partner. It is an international structural engineering consultancy that provides structural design and façade engineering services for a wide range of projects in locations including the UK, the USA, mainland Europe, the Middle and Far East, Russia, the Caribbean, from its main offices in New York and London. He works with leading architects on challenging structures of all kinds, and has headed the innovation of the use of glass, in works ranging from artworks and glass stairs, to the use of structural glass and large cable-hung glass walls in buildings.

In 2000 he was made an Honorary Fellow of the Royal Institute of British Architects and in 2003 was appointed to the Council of the Architectural Association School of Architecture. He was a member of the Design Review Committee of CABE 2000–03. In 2004 he was appointed to the RSA's Faculty of Royal Designers for Industry. He divides his time between the New York and London offices of the firm. For twenty years he has taught structures to architecture students, at architecture schools at the universities of Yale, Harvard, Princeton, London (the Bartlett); at the Architectural Association, Illinois Institute of Technology, The Rural Studio at Auburn University, and others.

Before forming his own consultancy in 1981, Tim Macfarlane worked with Alan Baxter Associates in London, following on from working with Charles Weiss & Partners and Arenco on major projects in the UK and Middle East. He graduated from Strathclyde University in 1974.

Carlos Jimenez

Carlos Jimenez, a native of Costa Rica, moved to the United States in 1974, graduated from the University of Houston School of Architecture in 1981, and established his own office in 1982. He has taught widely and held a number of endowed chair positions, including the first Favrot Chair in Architecture at Tulane University, the Eliot Noyes Visiting Design Professor at Harvard University, the Friedman Visiting Professor at the University of California at Berkeley, the Pietro Beluschi Chair at the University of Oregon, and the Ruth Carter Stevenson Professor at the University of Texas in Austin. He is a tenured professor at Rice University. He has won awards for excellence in design from Architectural Record, Progressive Architecture, and the Architectural League of New York, and has exhibited his work in museums and galleries across the country and abroad. His principal built works include the Administration and Junior School building for the Museum of Fine Arts Houston; the Spencer Studio Art Building at Williams College; the Cummins Child Development Center in Columbus, Indiana; the Peeler Art Center at DePauw University; and the Library Service Center for Rice University. His work is widely published, including three books and four monographic issues. He is currently a jury member of the Pritzker Architecture Prize.

Juhani Pallasmaa

Juhani Pallasmaa, who has practiced architecture since the early sixties, established his own office in Helsinki, Juhani Pallasmaa Architects, in 1983 after twenty years of collaboration with a number of architects. In addition to architectural design, he has been active in urban, product, and graphic design. He has taught and lectured widely in Europe, North and South America, Africa, and Asia, and published books and numerous essays on the philosophy and criticism of architecture and the arts in twenty languages. Pallasmaa has held positions as Professor at the Helsinki University of Technology (1991–97), State Artist Professor (1983–88), Director of the Museum of Finnish Architecture (1978–83), and Rector of the Institute of Industrial Arts, Helsinki (1970–71). He has held visiting professorships at Washington University in Saint Louis (1999–2004), the University of Virginia (1992), and Yale University (1993), and has taught and lectured in numerous universities, conferences, and symposia. His books include *Encounters: Architectural Essays 1976–2000* (Helsinki, 2004), *Sensuous Minimalism* (Beijing, 2002), *The Architecture of Image: Existential Space in Cinema* (Helsinki, 2001), *Alvar Aalto: Villa Mairea* (Helsinki, 1998), *The Eyes of the Skin* (London, 1996), *Animal Architecture* (Helsinki, 1995), *Maailmassaolon taide (The Art of Being-in-the-World: Essays on Art and Architecture;* Helsinki, 1993), *Alvar Aalto Furniture* (Helsinki and Cambridge, Mass., 1987), and *Language of Wood* (Helsinki, 1987).

Creative & Performing Arts High School

Camden, New Jersey

Designed 2003

Once home to shipbuilding, the poet Walt Whitman, and the RCA Victor corporation, Camden, New Jersey is now in the process of reinventing itself as a regional center for government, technology, health care, and education. As part of its program to promote all levels of education, and building on its artistic legacy, the Camden school district established a Creative and Performing Arts (CAPA) public magnet high school with an arts-oriented curriculum for 200 students. In addition to their regular academic studies, CAPA students elect "majors" of artistic emphasis such as drama, dance, creative writing, painting, sculpture, and choral or instrumental music. Already locally and internationally acclaimed performers, CAPA students also claim the district's highest graduation and college matriculation rates.

As part of a state-funded $8.6 billion campaign of new public school construction throughout New Jersey, Camden has planned to replace the CAPA's existing, outdated and inadequate building with a new, state of the art, 80,000-square-foot facility specifically designed to support and promote the school's curriculum. The new building will accommodate twice the current enrollment while providing facilities lacking in the existing building: a 425-seat professional-class auditorium, music ensemble and practice rooms, multimedia production and editing suites, art and dance studios, a media center, a multi-function gymnasium, outdoor performance and exhibit areas, as well as modern academic classrooms and science labs.

The new CAPA will occupy one of the city's most prominent blocks, adjacent to City Hall on downtown Camden's eastern edge. The site punctuates two urban axes extending eastward from the Delaware River: commercial Market Street and educational Cooper Street—home to a college, two universities, and two charter schools. From the west, the site serves as a highly visible local and regional gateway to Camden's central business district and waterfront attractions, with direct sightlines and connections to an adjacent highway and the Benjamin Franklin Bridge toll plaza, which motorists cross on their way to and from Philadelphia across the river.

The new building's design provides for a highly flexible arrangement of multi-function performance spaces which accommodate the school's existing arts programs while also inspiring new, impromptu, and as yet unforeseen uses by students, faculty, and the greater Camden community. The project uses a strictly limited budget and total building area as incentives for finding a greater performative efficiency, a means of allowing the curriculum to escape its formal organizational constraints into a field of maximized performative potential throughout the school campus. By using a system of flexible arrangements, strategic adjacencies, and rooms which may open to public spaces and the outdoors, the building allows formal performance spaces to expand as needed while also giving other spaces the ability to support creative activities as desired. This environment will inspire the continual re-investigation of creative production and performance space as well as the relationships between artist and audience, building and city, and school and community.

As an integral part of the CAPA design process, SOM has been working with the renowned film, video, and performance artist Robert Whitman. Whitman has been engaged in developing the above mentioned strategies for maximizing the school's performative potential—specifially, in terms of developing a flexible infrastructure deployed around the school and its grounds to allow any space to support and promote the widest range of creative activities.

1 Plan of downtown Camden, with major
  urban axes intersecting at project site
2 Aerial view from City Hall showing new
  building and front yard
3 Artist Robert Whitman during *News*
  performance in 2002
4 Publication from Robert Whitman's show at
  Dia Art Foundation, New York, 2003
5 *American Moon*, by Robert Whitman, 1960;
  final scene of performance

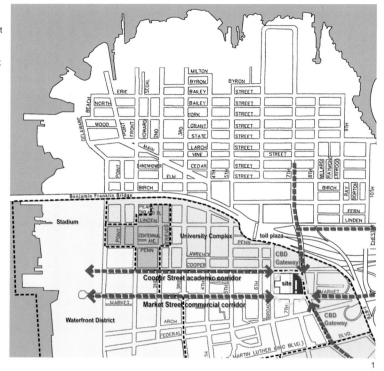

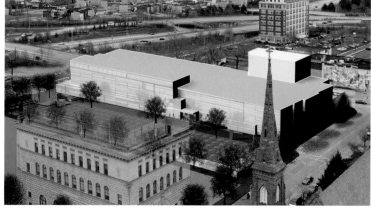

3

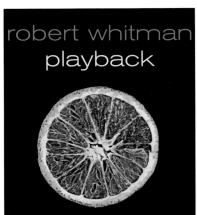

4

5

6 Work sessions with students, faculty,
   and artist Robert Whitman
7 Model with projections on and from the
   school that interact with the neighborhood

6

8 View of stage opening to amphitheater

9 View with exterior projections

10 View of main entrance with performance space

11 Front Yard Elevation

12 Haddon Avenue Elevation

13 Market Street Elevation

8

9

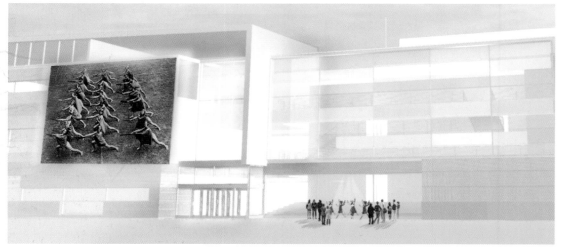

10

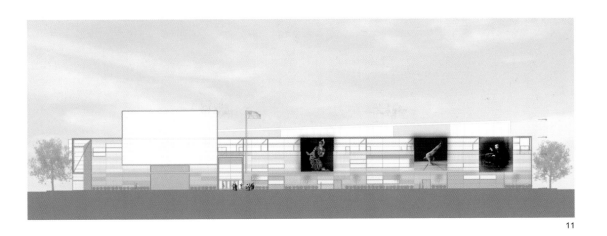

11

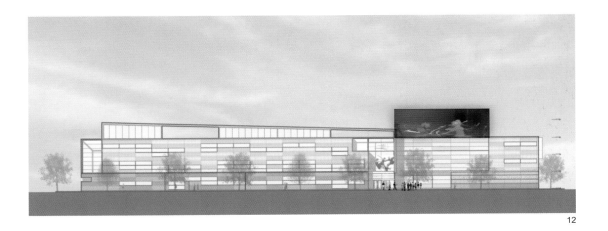

12

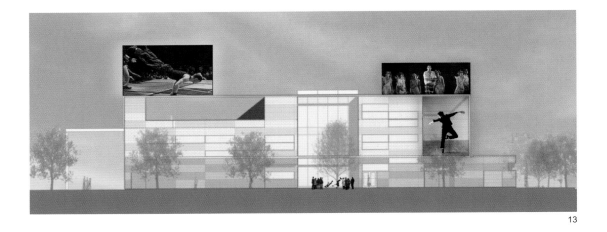

13

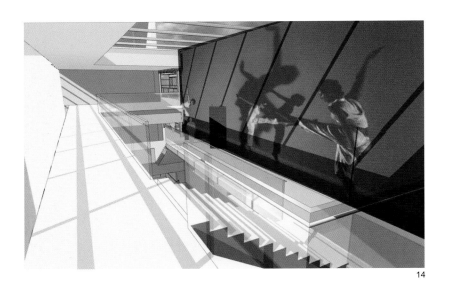

14

15

16

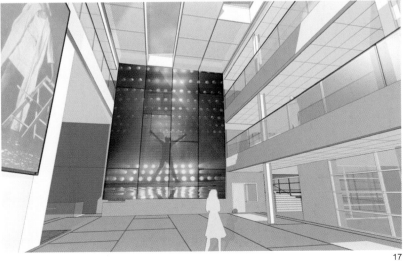

17

Schloss Velden

Carinthia, Austria

Designed 2004

Two goals were established as a precedent to the design of an addition to the historic Schloss Velden, made necessary by the requirement to accommodate a significant expansion of hotel and spa facilities: First, the original historic Schloss was to retain its iconic presence and dominant feature within the garden grounds; Second, the new structures necessary to accommodate the hotel, conference center, and spa program would be, to the greatest extent possible, indistinguishable from the gardens that surround the original Schloss.

If successful, the design of the project could offer a new view regarding the relationships between buildings and landscape as a reflection of an alternative regard for the relationship between man and nature. Additionally and as a consequence, a new hotel/spa typology would result from the subtle modifications to an existing context rather than the imposition of more traditional hotel/spa forms onto the landscape.

By "folding" the lawn surfaces within the gardens, the program is accommodated without the visible addition of "buildings." This approach to building "camouflage" makes ephemeral the boundary between building and garden. As a consequence, the historic Schloss maintains it preeminent stature within the grounds of the estate and focal point of the greatly enlarged complex.

The geometry of the folds emerges from the deformation of a grid representing longitudes and latitudes laid over the site. Specific deformations would reflect the volumes required to accommodate various program elements. The resulting irregular deformations are intentional attempts to further camouflage the program within the context of a 19th-century Romantic landscape.

In addition to the more common approaches to sustainable design, the scheme introduces new notions of sustainability, where beyond an empirical evaluation of "green," there is also an emphasis on visual and cultural sustainability.

1

2

3

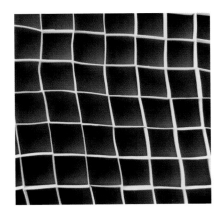

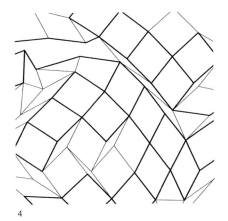

4

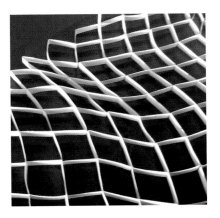

5

hotel unterer park level
1:200

1 gourmet restaurant
2 vorbereitungsbereich
3 hotelbar
4 rezeption restaurant
5 personalbüro
6 terrasse orangerie / hotelbar
7 foyer orangerie /
  hotelerweiterung
8 orangerie restaurant
9 orangerie loungebar
10 kellner vorbereitungsraum

6

7

6 Hotel plan

7 Hotel interior perspective

8 Hotel model view 1

9 Hotel model view 2

8

9

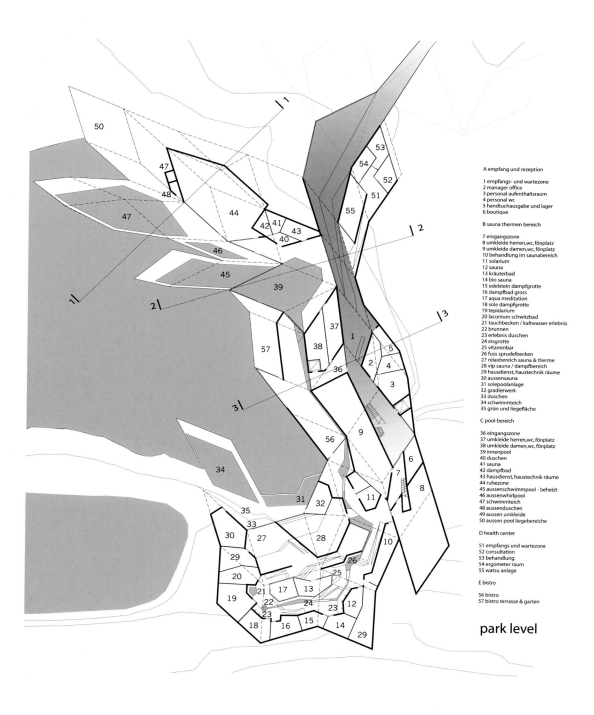

A empfang und rezeption

1 empfangs- und wartezone
2 manager office
3 personal aufenthaltsraum
4 personal wc
5 handtuchausgabe und lager
6 boutique

B sauna thermen bereich

7 eingangszone
8 umkleide herren,wc, fönplatz
9 umkleide damen,wc, fönplatz
10 behandlung im saunabereich
11 solarium
12 sauna
13 kräuterbad
14 bio sauna
15 edelstein dampfgrotte
16 dampfbad gross
17 aqua meditation
18 sole dampfgrotte
19 tepidarium
20 laconium schwitzbad
21 tauchbecken / kaltwasser erlebnis
22 brunnen
23 erlebnis duschen
24 eisgrotte
25 vitaminbar
26 fuss sprudelbecken
27 relaxbereich sauna & therme
28 vip sauna / dampfbereich
29 hausdienst, haustechnik räume
30 aussensauna
31 solepoolanlage
32 gradierwerk
33 duschen
34 schwimmteich
35 grün und liegefläche

C pool bereich

36 eingangszone
37 umkleide herren,wc, fönplatz
38 umkleide damen,wc, fönplatz
39 innenpool
40 duschen
41 sauna
42 dampfbad
43 hausdienst, haustechnik räume
44 ruhezone
45 aussenschwimmpool - beheizt
46 aussenwhirlpool
47 schwimmteich
48 aussenduschen
49 aussen umkleide
50 aussen pool liegebereiche

D health center

51 empfangs und wartezone
52 consultation
53 behandlung
54 ergometer raum
55 watsu anlage

E bistro

56 bistro
57 bistro terrasse & garten

park level

10 Spa plan
11 Spa exterior perspective
12 Spa interior perspective

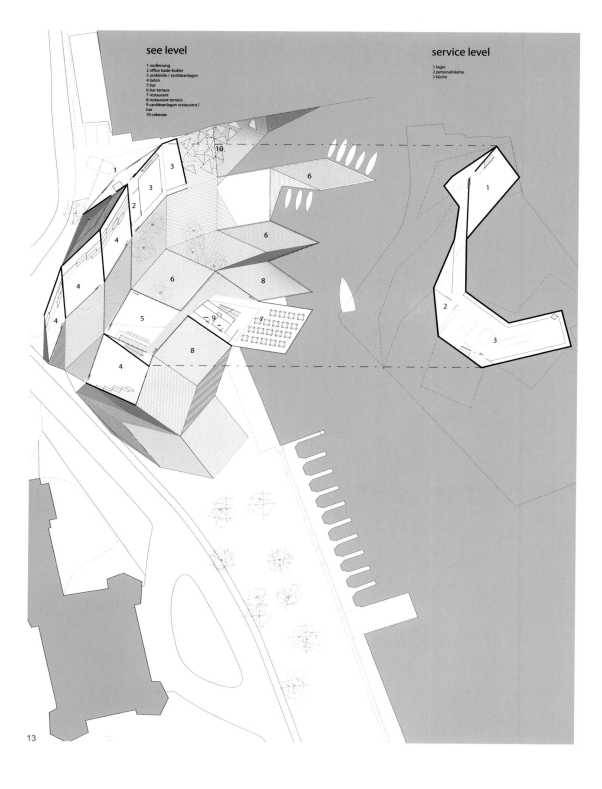

see level

1 andienung
2 office bade-butler
3 umkleide / sanitäranlagen
4 laden
5 bar
6 bar terrace
7 restaurant
8 restaurant terrace
9 sanitäranlagen restaurant /
bar
10 cabanas

service level

1 lager
2 personalräume
3 küche

13

13 Beach club plan

14 Beach club exterior perspective

15 Restaurant interior perspective

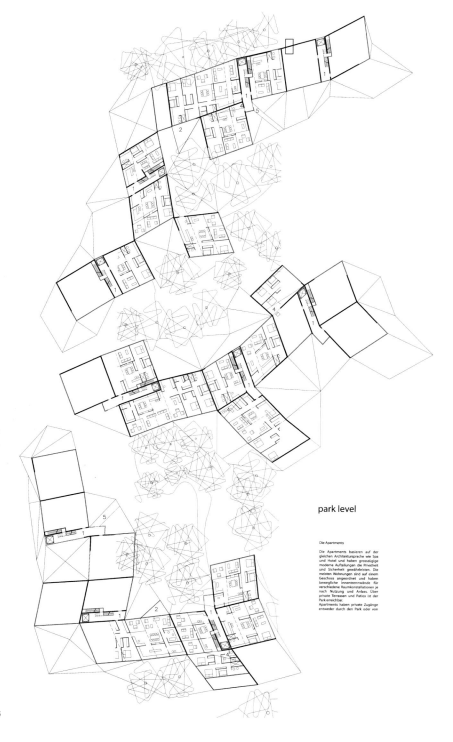

park level

Die Apartments

Die Apartments basieren auf der
gleichen Architektursprache wie Spa
und Hotel und haben grosszügige
moderne Aufteilungen die Privatheit
und Sicherheit gewährleisten. Die
meisten Wohnungen sind auf einem
Geschoss angeordnet und haben
bewegliche Innentrennwände für
verschiedene Raumkonstellationen je
nach Nutzung und Anlass. Über
private Terrassen und Patios ist der
Park erreichbar.
Apartments haben private Zugänge
entweder durch den Park oder von

16 Residence plans

17 Apartment interior plan

18 Volume deformation model

19 Flocking diagram

19

18

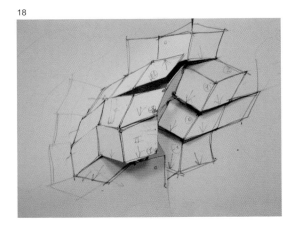

Top: Kobe Quake, Japan, Jan. 17, 1995. Lower left: San Salvador Quake, El Salvador, Oct. 10, 1986. Lower right: Michoacan Quake, Mexico, Sept. 19, 1985

Pin-Fuse Joint™

US Patent No. 6,681,538 B1

Date of Patent: January 27, 2004

Ensuring life safety in structures during and after a seismic event is an architect's and engineer's primary goal. However, the economic viability of structures following the event is crucial to initial business investment decisions and long-term business successes. If structures were capable of resisting potentially destructive earthquake forces while altering their characteristics without permanent deformation, the structure would not only be safe but also economically superior.

Structures designed and built in regions of high seismicity are conceived with juxtaposing criteria. They must be designed for strength, providing enough resistance to protect life safety and avoid collapse. However, they must be designed economically, using inherent ductility to dissipate energy by means of reasonably sized structural members. Traditionally, structural steel building frames have utilized beam-to-column moment connections that are welded with the frame beams perpendicular to the columns. Beams connected to the face of columns rotate when subjected to racking of the building frame. These beams are designed to protect the column integrity and prevent potential collapse by plastically deforming during frame motion. This deformation, however, likely decreases post-earthquake integrity and economic viability in the process.

Following the 1994 Northridge earthquake in California, designers, academicians, and building owners found the conventionally designed steel beam-to-columns moment connections protected life safety but in many cases resulted in unsuccessful investment because of failed joints (cracked welds, cracked steel sections, etc.) and permanent building deformations. With future performance questionable and repairs difficult, the design and construction industry searched for more reliable solutions. Many solutions were proposed and developed. Some patents were awarded. These solutions varied from strongly reinforcing the beam-to-column joint with welded plates to creating slots in the moment-resisting beam webs to reducing the flange sections of the beams at the joint (The "Dogbone"). However, none of these solutions addressed the fundamental behavior issue of eliminating plastic (permanent yielding) deformations. In addition, none addressed the natural rotation requirements of the joints that must provide resistance as well as must provide a controlled release of energy when forces are excessive.

The Pin-Fuse Joint™ allows building movement caused by a seismic event while maintaining structural elasticity after strong ground motion. The joint introduces a circular-plated end connection for the steel beams framing into the steel or composite columns within a moment-resisting frame. Slip-critical friction-type bolts connect the curved steel end plates. A steel pin or hollow steel pipe in the center of the moment-frame beam provides a well-defined rotation point. Under typical service conditions including wind and moderate seismic events, the joint remains fixed where applied forces do not overcome the friction resistance provided between the curved end plates. However, during an extreme event, the joint is designed to rotate around the pin joint, with the slip-critical bolts sliding in long-slotted holes in the curved end plates. With this slip, rotation is allowed, energy dissipated, and "fusing" occurs.

The rotation of the Pin-Fuse Joint™ during extreme seismic events occurs sequentially in designated locations within the frame. As the slip occurs, the building frame is softened. The dynamic characteristics of the frame are altered with a lengthening of the building period, less forces are attracted by the frame; however, no inelastic deformation is realized. After the seismic event, the elastic frame finds its pre-earthquake, natural-centered position. The brass shim located between the curved steel plates provides a predictable coefficient of friction required to determine the onset of slip and enables the bolts to maintain their tension and consequently the clamping force after the earthquake has subsided.

Conventional structural steel moment-resisting frame

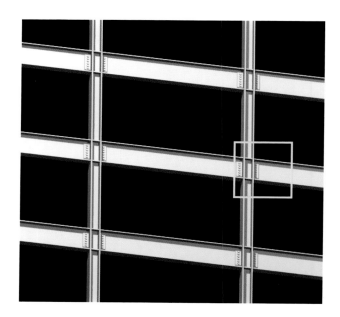

Conventional Beam-to-Column Joint

(Pre-Northridge Connection)

- Beam flanges fully welded and beam web bolted
  to column at joint;
- limited ductility;
- plastic (permanent) deformations expected
  after medium-level earthquake.

Dogbone or Reduced Beam Section

(Post-Northridge Connection)

- Beam fully welded to column at joint with
  partial removal of beam flanges;
- good ductility;
- plastic (permanent) deformations expected
  after medium-level earthquake.

Structural steel moment-resisting frame
illustrating locations of the Pin-Fuse Joint™

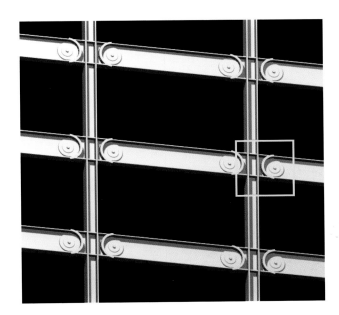

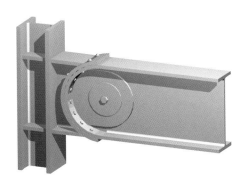

Pin-Fuse Joint™

- Curved structural steel end plates bolted together
  with friction connection;
- pin placed in beam web to created center of rotation;
- no plastic (permanent) deformations even after
  extreme seismic event.

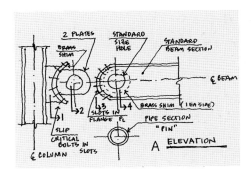

First concept sketch, Feb. 12, 2002

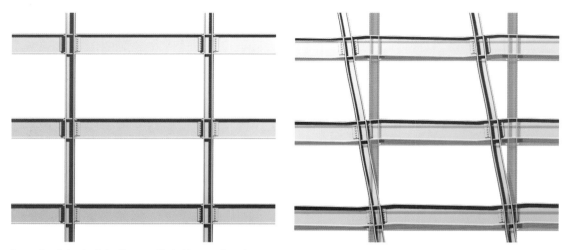

Conventional structural steel frame subjected to an earthquake

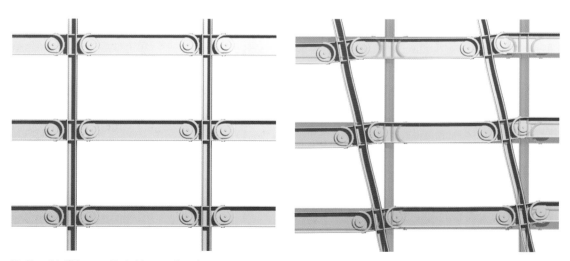

Pin-Fuse Joint™ frame subjected to an earthquake

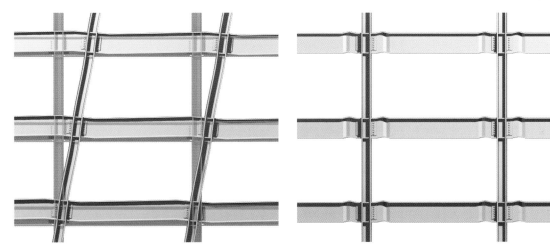

Steel frame compromised after earthquake

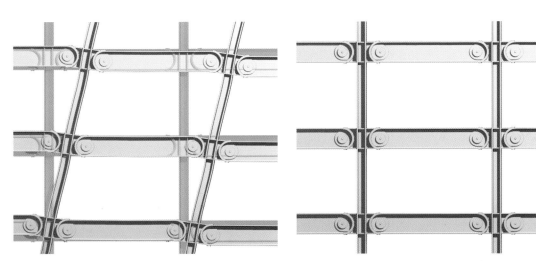

Steel frame intact without permanent deformations after earthquake

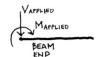

$V_{APPLIED}$

$M_{APPLIED}$

BEAM
END

$V_{APPLIED} = V_{GRAVITY} \mp V_{SEISMIC}$

$M_{APPLIED} = M_{GRAVITY} \pm M_{SEISMIC}$

PIN-FUSE JOINT WILL ONLY
ROTATE WHEN APPLIED
BENDING MOMENT IN FRAME
BEAM OVERCOMES RESISTING
MOMENT DEVELOPED BY
THE INDIVIDUAL SHEAR
RESISTANCE OF HIGH-STRENGTH
BOLTS RADIALLY PLACED ABOUT
THE JOINT'S CENTER OF
ROTATION

AS JOINT ROTATES, ENERGY IS
DISSIPATED THROUGH CURVED
SLIP PLANE. THE FRAME
SOFTENS, BUILDING PERIOD
LENGTHENS, LESS FORCE FROM
GROUND MOTION IS ATTRACTED
BY FRAME.

DISPLACEMENT OF FRAME IS
DESIGNED SO JOINT ROTATION
NEVER EXCEEDS LENGTH OF
TRAVEL IN SLOTTED BOLT
CONNECTIONS.

AFTER MOVEMENT, BOLT TENSION
REMAINS AND COEFFICIENT OF
STATIC FRICTION IS RE-ESTABLISH-
ED. MOMENT RESISTANCE
REMAINS FOR NEXT SEISMIC
EVENT

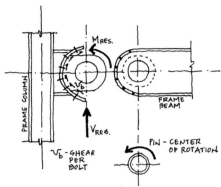

FRAME COLUMN

$M_{RES.}$

V_b

$V_{RES.}$

FRAME
BEAM

V_b - SHEAR
PER
BOLT

PIN - CENTER
OF ROTATION

$V_{RES.} = V_{RESISTING} \Rightarrow$ WEB PIN

$M_{RES.} = M_{RESISTING} \Rightarrow$ SLIP CRITICAL
BOLTS SUBJECTED
TO SHEAR WHEN
ROTATION OCCURS

SLIP ONLY OCCURS WHEN :

$M_{APPLIED} > M_{RES.} = \mu N n \frac{d}{2}$

GRAVITY +
SEISMIC

$N =$ NORMAL FRICTION FORCE DUE
TO TENSION IN BOLT BASED ON
TORQUE REQ'D TO ACHIEVE SLIP CRITICAL
CONN. (A325/A490 BOLTS AND DEPENDENT
ON DIAMETER)

$n = \#$ OF BOLTS

$\frac{d}{2} =$ DEPTH OF FRAME BEAM DIVIDED BY 2

$\mu = 0.3$ (APPROX.) FOR STEEL PLATE/BRASS SHIM
INTERFACE

$F = \mu N$

$F =$ FORCE TO CAUSE SLIP

$\mu =$ COEF. OF FRICTION

$N =$ NORMAL FORCE (FORCE
APPLIED DUE TO TENSION
IN BOLTS)

1

2

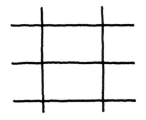

UNDEFORMED SHAPE

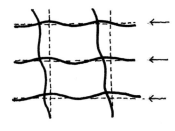

DEFORMED SHAPE
DUE TO SEISMIC LOADING

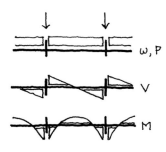

APPLIED LOADS, SHEARS &
BENDING MOMENTS DUE TO
GRAVITY EFFECTS ON FRAME

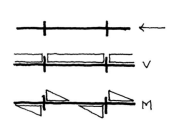

APPLIED LOADS, SHEARS &
BENDING MOMENTS DUE TO
SEISMIC EFFECTS ON FRAME

3

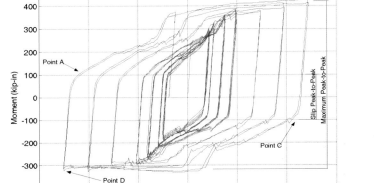

1 Stuctural concept for Pin-Fuse Joint™
2 Specimen testing at Stanford University
3 Frame force diagrams
4 Moment-rotation relationship graph

4

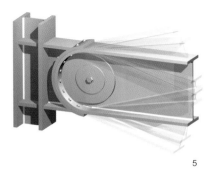

5

5 The Pin-Fuse Joint™ elastically designed for
a 3% rotation at a 475-year seismic event

6 Assembly and construction of the Pin-Fuse Joint™ System

  a) Pre-fabricated column and beam units

  b) Fit-up unit and install brass shims

  c) Install flange friction bolts and web pin

  d) Install mid-span beam splice in erected building frame

7 Upwardly rotated position

8 At-rest position

9 Downwardly rotated position

10 The Pin-Fuse Joint™ model

6a

b

c

d

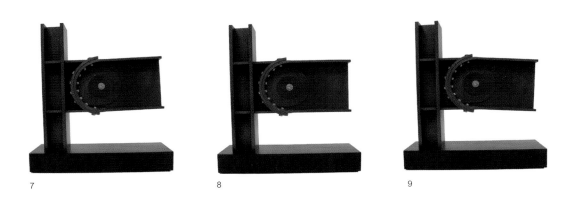

7   8   9

10

US006681538B1

(12) **United States Patent**   (10) **Patent No.:   US 6,681,538 B1**
Sarkisian   (45) **Date of Patent: Jan. 27, 2004**

(54)	**SEISMIC STRUCTURAL DEVICE**

(75) Inventor: **Mark P. Sarkisian**, San Anselmo, CA (US)

(73) Assignee: **Skidmore, Owings & Merrill LLP**, New York, NY (US)

(*) Notice: Subject to any disclaimer, the term of this patent is extended or adjusted under 35 U.S.C. 154(b) by 1 day.

(21) Appl. No.: **10/200,679**

(22) Filed: **Jul. 22, 2002**

(51) Int. Cl.⁷ **E04B 7/00**

(52) **U.S. Cl.** **52/289**; 52/702; 52/167.1; 52/283; 403/335; 403/337

(58) **Field of Search** 52/167.1, 283, 52/289, 702, 736.2; 403/335, 336, 337, 338, 257, 258, 83, 84, 87; 248/250

(56)   **References Cited**

U.S. PATENT DOCUMENTS

3,938,294	A		2/1976	Gaburri 52/743
3,974,614	A		8/1976	Strong 52/573
4,041,659	A	*	8/1977	McElhoe 52/93.1
4,054,392	A	*	10/1977	Oppenheim 403/175
4,091,594	A	*	5/1978	Yamashita 52/737.2
4,344,716	A	*	8/1982	Sigal 403/13
4,348,129	A	*	9/1982	Conforti 403/218
4,615,157	A	*	10/1986	Murray 52/167.4
4,658,556	A	*	4/1987	Jenkins 52/317
4,779,484	A	*	10/1988	Poe 74/608
4,781,003	A		11/1988	Rizza 52/396
4,922,667	A		5/1990	Kobori et al. 52/167
4,928,930	A	*	5/1990	Chung 256/67
5,319,907	A		6/1994	Nicholas et al. 52/396.05
5,408,798	A		4/1995	Hohmann 52/562
5,491,941	A		2/1996	Lancelot, III 52/223.9
5,537,790	A		7/1996	Jackson 52/393

5,797,227	A		8/1998	Garza-Tamez 52/167.1
5,875,598	A		3/1999	Batten et al. 52/396.01
6,101,780	A		8/2000	Kreidt 52/712
6,102,627	A	*	8/2000	Ueda et al. 405/255
6,115,972	A		9/2000	Tamez 52/167.4
6,185,897	B1		2/2001	Johnson et al. 52/583.1
6,237,292	B1		5/2001	Hegemier et al. 52/273
6,289,640	B1		9/2001	Ueda et al. 52/167.9
6,324,795	B1		12/2001	Stiles et al. 52/167.4
2001/0045069	A1		11/2001	Constantinou 52/167.3
2002/0184836	A1	*	12/2002	Takeuchi et al.

* cited by examiner

Primary Examiner—Carl D. Friedman
Assistant Examiner—Nahid Amiri
(74) *Attorney, Agent, or Firm*—Sonnenschein, Nath & Rosenthal LLP

(57)   **ABSTRACT**

The present invention is a pin-fuse joint generally utilized in a beam-to-column joint assembly subject to extreme seismic loading. The pin-fuse joint resists bending moments and shears generated by these loads. The joint is comprised of standard structural steel building materials, but may be applied to structures comprised of structural steel, reinforced concrete, and or composite materials, e.g., a combination of structural steel and reinforced concrete. The beam-to-column assembly is comprised of a column and a beam and a plate assembly that extends between the column and the beam. The plate assembly is welded to the column and is attached to the beam via the pin-fuse joint. The pin fuse joint is created by a pin connection through the beam and the connection plates of the plate assembly at the web of the beam. Additionally, both the plate assembly and the beam have curved flange end connectors that sit flush against one another separated only by a brass shim when the beam and plate assembly are joined. The curved flange end connectors of the beam and plate assembly are then secured against one another by torqued high-strength bolts.

13 Claims, 7 Drawing Sheets

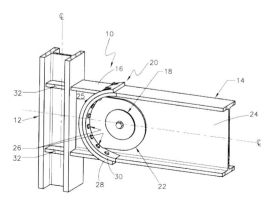

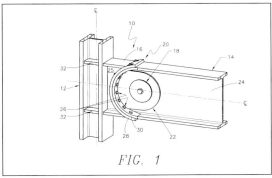

FIG. 1

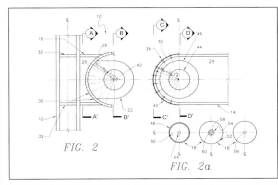

FIG. 2

FIG. 2a

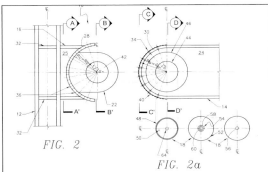

FIG. 2

FIG. 2a

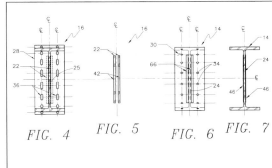

FIG. 4   FIG. 5   FIG. 6   FIG. 7

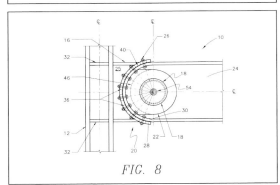

FIG. 8

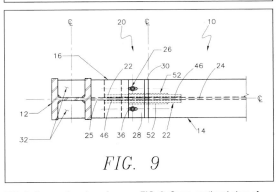

FIG. 9

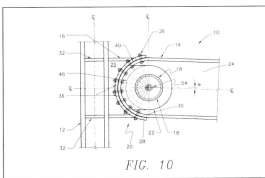

FIG. 10

FIG. 1 Perspective view of one embodiment of a beam-to-column joint assembly

FIG. 2 Exploded front view of beam-to-column joint assembly

FIG. 2a Front view of a pipe/pin assembly and web stiffener used to connect the moment-resisting beam to the plate assembly

FIG. 3 Exploded top view of beam-to-column joint assembly

FIG. 4 Cross sectional view of plate assembly (Fig. 2) taken along line A-A

FIG. 5 Cross sectional view of plate assembly (Fig. 2) taken along line B-B

FIG. 6 Cross sectional view of moment-resisting beam (Fig. 2) taken along line C-C

FIG. 7 Cross sectional view of moment-resisting beam (Fig. 2) taken along line D-D

FIG. 8 Front view of one embodiment of beam-to-column joint assembly

FIG. 9 Top view of one embodiment of beam-to-column joint assembly

FIG. 10 Perspective view of beam-to-column joint assembly as it would appear with pin-fuse joint rotated when subject to extreme loading conditions

ARB Bank Headquarters

Riyadh, Saudi Arabia

Designed 2003–04

ARB is conceived as a series of earth-forms within an active farmland that will change with seasons. Cultivating the land amidst the desert landscape creates a strong sense of place and identity for the bank.

The centerpiece of the project is a cistern, where the water is collected, controlled and distributed. A 60-meter tall, monolithic rammed earth cube rises from the cistern. The walls of the monolith act as a protective envelope against harsh Middle Eastern climatic elements such as sun, wind, sand, and urban conditions like noise and blast. Rammed earth construction, the technique of pounding moist earth into a formwork to create monolithic walls of earth, has been used for thousands of years. This traditional construction technique allows the use of inexpensive local materials in a thick walled system that maintains a high thermal mass leading to lower energy use. Within these protective earth walls an internal labyrinth of interconnected program elements is located.

The project challenges the preconceived notion of office building typology by dividing its internalized office components vertically into three vertical precincts, yet weaving them back together with a complex tissue of open spaces. The interlocked arrangement of the precinct creates a series of courtyards to maximize the interaction. A spiraling ramp that runs along the monolithic walls weaves together the interconnected courtyards and precincts.

The monolithic walls are penetrated by a sequence of "periscoping-windows." The periscoping-window is an armature to control light & views, which allows one to see without being seen, a widely used concept in the Middle East in order to protect privacy. The windows create a phenomenal play of light and shadow, and allow intermittent glimpses of outside views as one moves along the spiraling ramp.

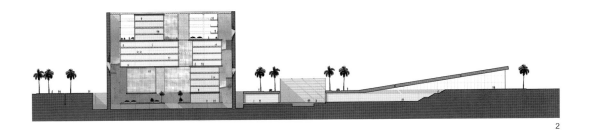

2

3

1 Massing model

2 Site section

3 Site plan

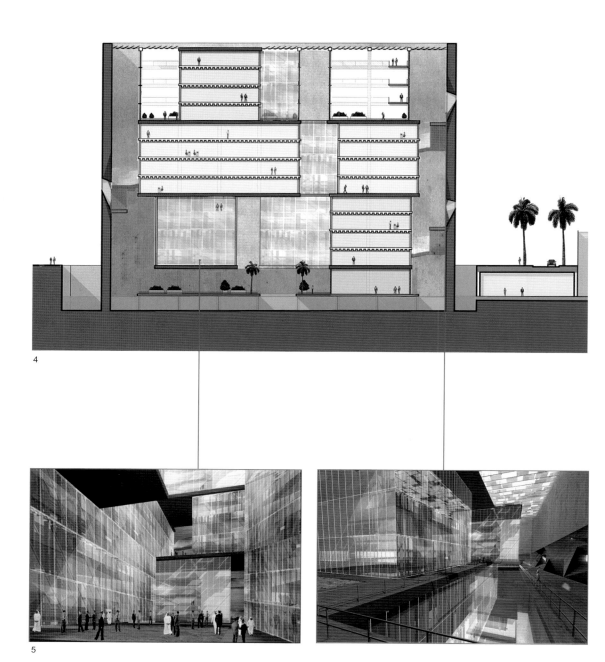

4

5

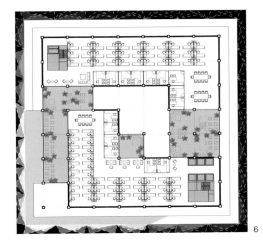

6

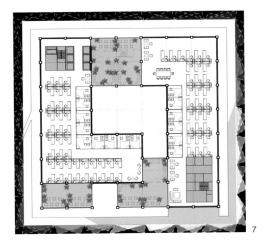

7

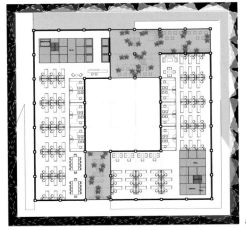

8

WEST   NORTH

9 Unfolded interior elevations

10 Light variations through periscoping windows

11 Axonometric

12 Perspective

13 Periscoping window diagrams

>14 View from inside monolith wall

>15 Model elevation

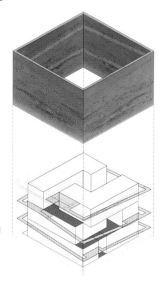

11

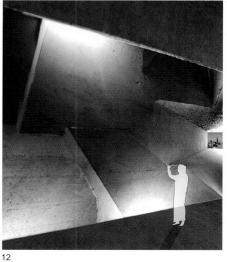

12

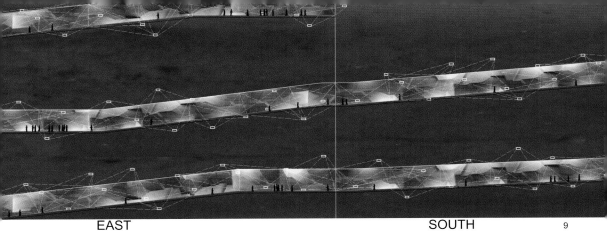

EAST   SOUTH   9

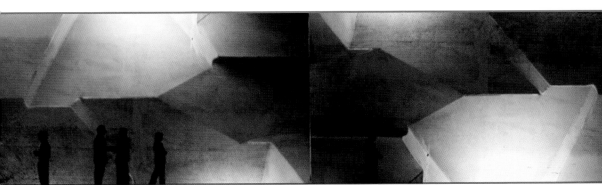

10

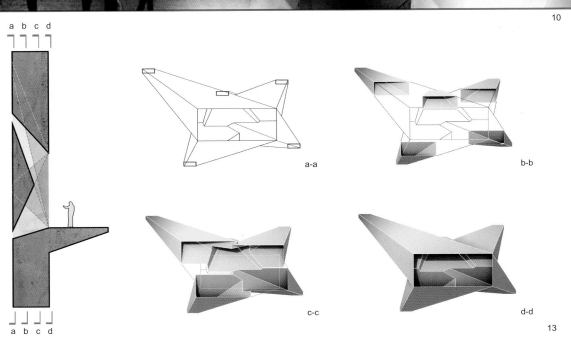

a b c d

a-a

b-b

c-c

d-d

a b c d

13

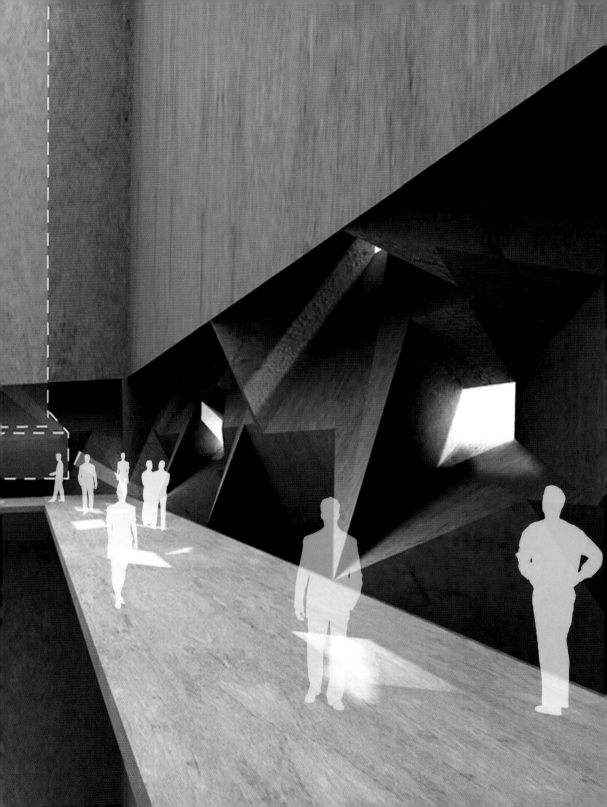

United States Air Force Academy
Cadet Chapel Restoration
Colorado Springs, Colorado
Designed 2003–04

The Cadet Chapel at the United States Air Force Academy was originally designed by SOM in 1957 as part of the master plan and design of the entire academy campus. Originally the Cadet Chapel took seven years to design and construct amid much public debate. When finally completed in 1963, it became the first SOM project credited to a single designer: Walter Netsch. In the spring of 1956, Walter took several weeks to cross Europe in search of inspiring precedents. He found inspiration at St. Francis of Assisi, La Sainte-Chapelle, and Chartres Cathedral. He remarked: "I came home with this tremendous feeling of how can I, in this modern age of technology, create something that will be inspiring and aspiring as Chartres, with both the light of La Sainte-Chapelle and of Chartres." For Walter, Chartres Cathedral embodied "a sense of place, as it could be seen from a distance arising over the wheat fields, similar to the Academy out in the middle of nowhere."

Inspired by ecclesiastical icons of the Middle Ages, the Cadet Chapel has become itself an icon of the Modern Age. The Chapel was designed to be provocative and iconic, and symbolic to the mission of the newly created Air Force. Its design forged ahead in form and materials from the typical building conventions of the time. Many of the design details of the building pre-dated technological advances in materials and methods that would have made the exterior a more robust system. Unlike fighter jets, the Cadet Chapel has gone forty years without evolving with new technology.

On the eve of the 50th anniversary of the United States Air Force Academy, SOM was approached to pursue a restoration design for the Cadet Chapel that would fix problems of water infiltration, repair any deteriorated components, remove any added elements, and restore the chapel to its original form and detailed profiles. In 2003 a complete investigation was conducted to analyze specific problem areas, deteriorated components, and to learn more about the building's complexities in order to design a successful solution.

This icon, dynamically designed with progressive materials and systems of its times, has now fallen behind contemporary technological standards. Due to value engineering of the cladding system the enclosure began to suffer from water intrusion. Over the years, the Academy has implemented short-term and low-cost remediations that have not only failed to enhance the performance of the exterior wall, but have also negatively impacted the aesthetics. The addition of a rain gutter with downspouts at the middle of the A-frame has visually cut the soaring spires in half. A wire-glass storm sash placed over the stained glass strip windows has greatly obscured their colorizing effect, and annual resealing of all the joints with low performing urethane sealant has stained the aluminum panels. The Chapel's original exterior was a single barrier system against the weather, while the repairs in the late 20th century were patches to fix any leakage. The current design inserts a sub-frame and weather barrier layer under the exterior panels, which are to be employed as a rain screen in a pressure equalized system. This is consistent with the philosophy of previous SOM modernist restorations: to employ state of the art systems and material to preserve the profiles and original design intent.

The Project Goals were defined as:

1. Restore exterior enclosure to original design profiles and visible materials

2. Introduce contemporary exterior enclosure concepts and systems to improve exterior performance

3. Restore the interior space to its original visual brilliance and maintain its visceral spirituality

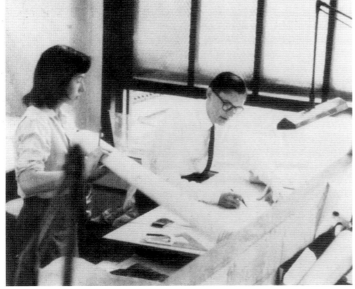

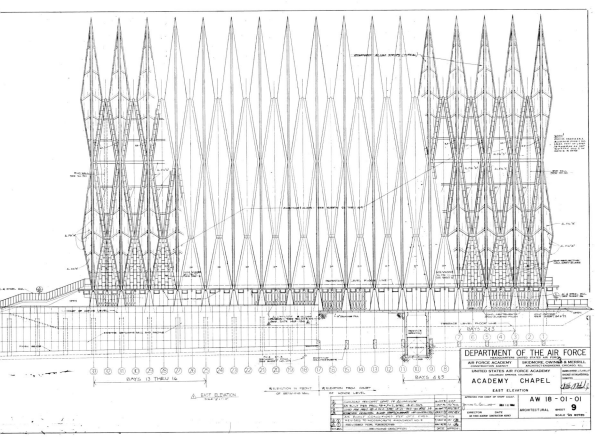

3

95

Renovation History

7

8

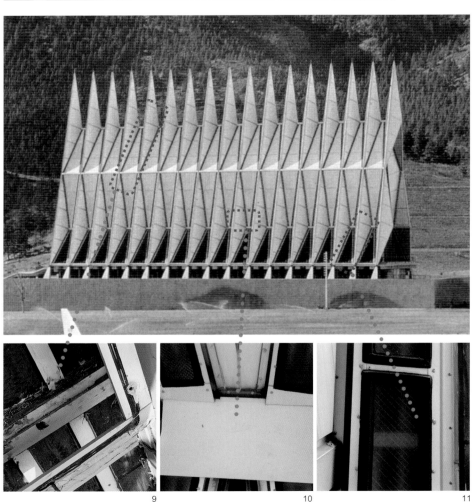

9

10

11

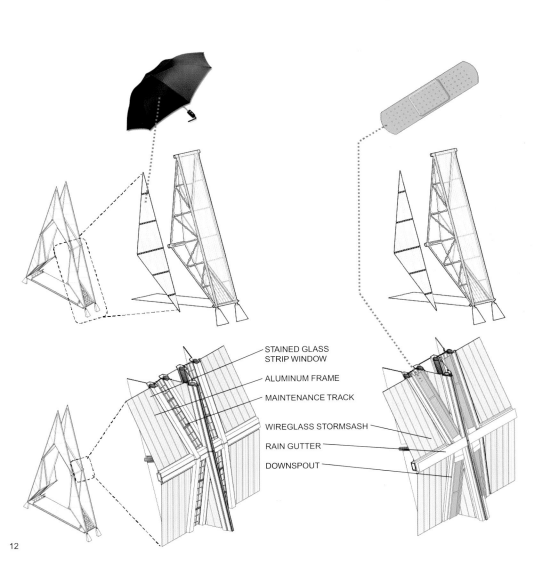

STAINED GLASS
STRIP WINDOW

ALUMINUM FRAME

MAINTENANCE TRACK

WIREGLASS STORMSASH

RAIN GUTTER

DOWNSPOUT

12

13

14

13 Extruded aluminum panel and frame removed
during intrusive investigation

14 Revealed steel frame during intrusive investigation

15 Discontinuous flashing at steel frame connection

16 Image showing interior of tetrahedron with aluminum
panel removed

17 Multi-directional anchor failure

15

16

17

"Wrap & Boot" Flashing

Secondary Air and Moisture Barrier

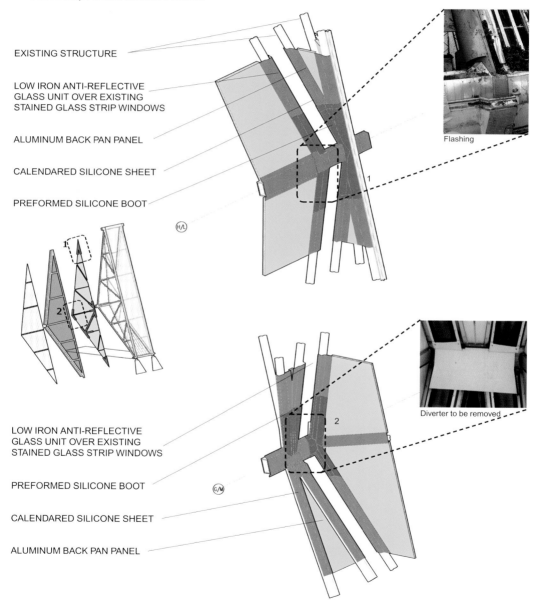

EXISTING STRUCTURE

LOW IRON ANTI-REFLECTIVE
GLASS UNIT OVER EXISTING
STAINED GLASS STRIP WINDOWS

ALUMINUM BACK PAN PANEL

CALENDARED SILICONE SHEET

PREFORMED SILICONE BOOT

Flashing

LOW IRON ANTI-REFLECTIVE
GLASS UNIT OVER EXISTING
STAINED GLASS STRIP WINDOWS

PREFORMED SILICONE BOOT

CALENDARED SILICONE SHEET

ALUMINUM BACK PAN PANEL

Diverter to be removed

Restoration Design 2004
Pressure Equalized System

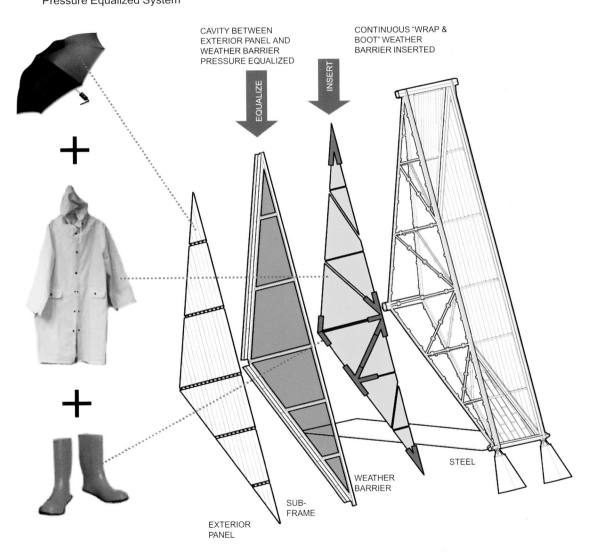

CAVITY BETWEEN EXTERIOR PANEL AND WEATHER BARRIER PRESSURE EQUALIZED

CONTINUOUS "WRAP & BOOT" WEATHER BARRIER INSERTED

EQUALIZE

INSERT

EXTERIOR PANEL

SUB-FRAME

WEATHER BARRIER

STEEL

West Bay Office Tower

Doha, Qatar

Designed 2004

The West Bay Office Tower has been designed for a site on the outskirts of the city of Doha, Qatar. The other buildings nearby include hotels, high-rise residential buildings, and other offices. The project would enjoy views of the Persian Gulf and good proximity to central Doha. Our goal in designing the project was to create a building that responded to the harsh desert climate in an environmentally appropriate way.

The stone clad concrete structure of the building has been designed using a computerized optimization program that minimizes the use of material for the most efficient and economical configuration. The diagonal members become more slender but more frequent on the higher floors of the tower. The oval floor plate encloses the conditioned volume with the minimum amount of surface area. Curtain wall mullions are placed on a uniform 1.5-meter module that is independent of the building structure. The clear glass wall encloses an efficient centralized core with flexible lease spans.

The design maximizes the use of daylight while avoiding heat gain and glare through the introduction of a sun-shade/light shelf on each floor. The enclosure of the office is placed eccentrically within the structural cage to allow the light shelf to vary in depth on an arc defined by the path of the sun. It is deepest on the east and west elevations, shallower on the south and diminishes to nothing on the north, where no shading is required. The parabolic profile of the shelf allows an even glow of daylight to extend across the ceiling to the building core, while blocking direct light for most of the day

A dynamic landscape that incorporates pedestrian paths, a vehicular drop off, a café, health club, and covered parking greets visitors to the building. The glass walls of the three-story lobby allow this landscape to flow across the site. Vectors of movement through and around the site define the form of the landscape. It gives the site a unique sculptural quality and attempts to convey the impact of the building structure on the ground.

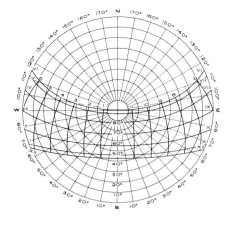

1

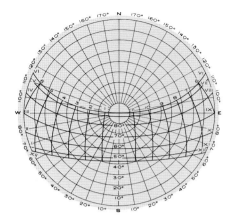

2

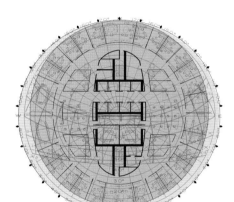

3

4

1 Sun diagram

   25deg 15min N longitude

   51deg 34 min E latitude

2 Exterior perimeter diagram

3 Ovular glass envelope diagram

4 Tower plan (typical)

5 Exterior perspective diagram

6 Exterior perspective diagram

7 Exterior wall section

5   6

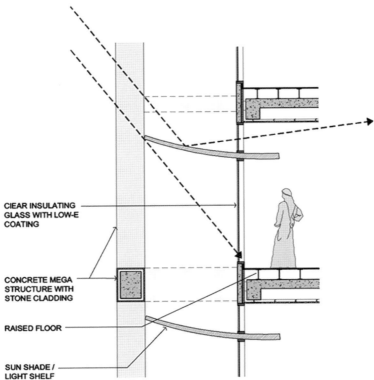

CIEAR INSULATING
GLASS WITH LOW-E
COATING

CONCRETE MEGA
STRUCTURE WITH
STONE CLADDING

RAISED FLOOR

7

SUN SHADE /
LIGHT SHELF

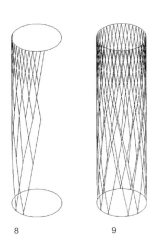

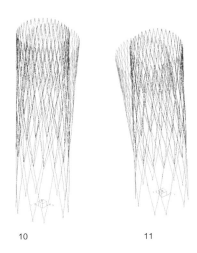

8   9   10   11

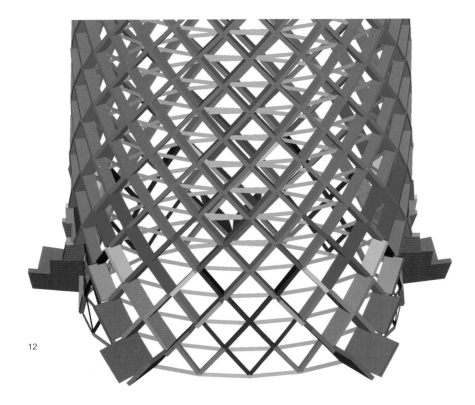

12

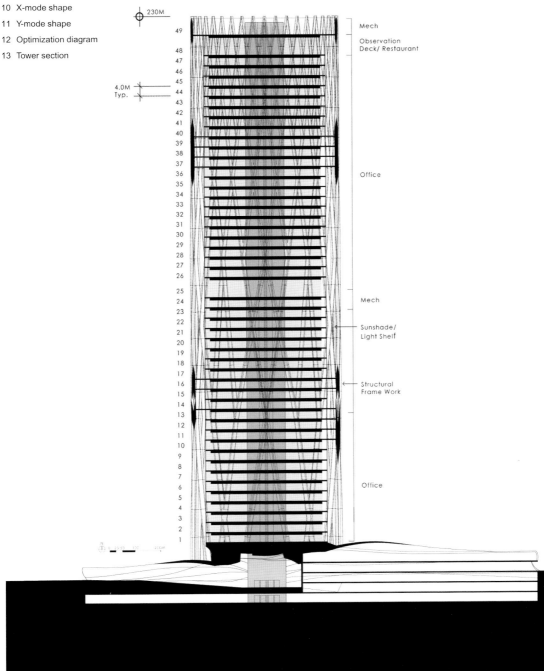

230M

4.0M
Typ.

49   Mech
      Observation
48   Deck/ Restaurant
47
46
45
44
43
42
41
40
39
38
37
36   Office
35
34
33
32
31
30
29
28
27
26
25
24   Mech
23
22
21   Sunshade/
20   Light Shelf
19
18
17
16   Structural
15   Frame Work
14
13
12
11
10
9
8
7
6   Office
5
4
3
2
1

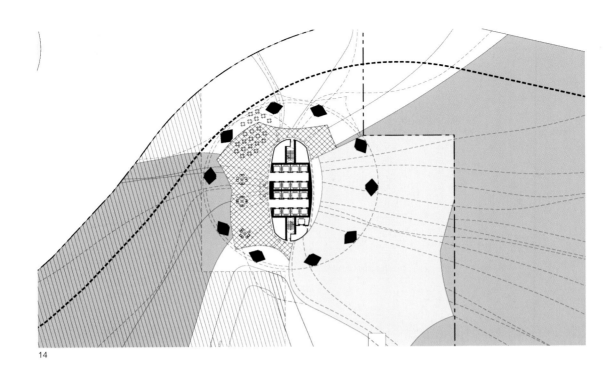

14

15

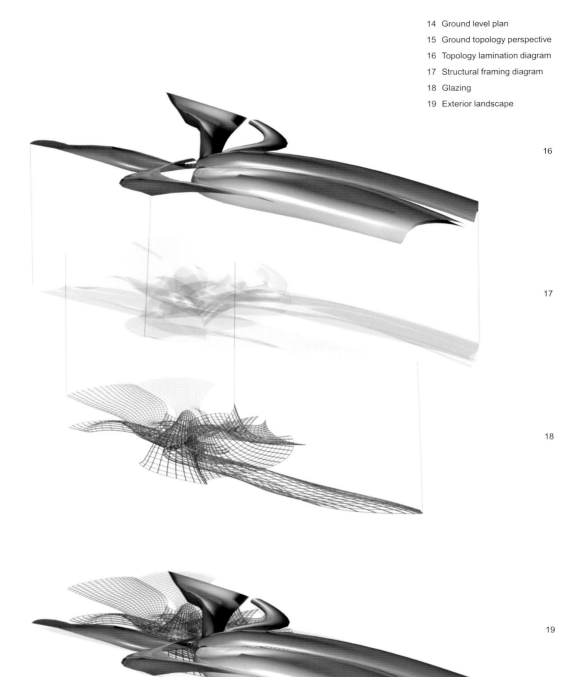

16

17

18

19

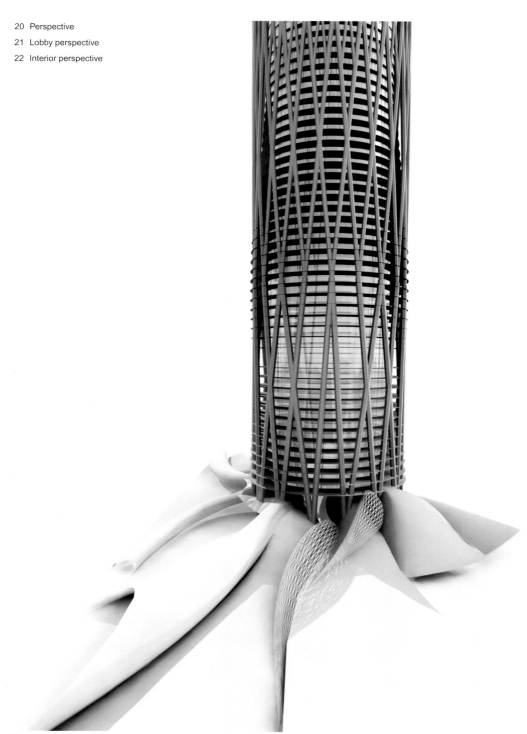

Office Interior Perspective

Project Updates

From *SOM Journal* 3

7 World Trade Center

New York, NY
Construction 2002–06

The first new building to rise on the World Trade Center site, 7 World Trade Center was completed in May of 2006. Construction of the podium began in May of 2002, driven by an immediate need to replace damaged Con Edison transformer vaults. The accelerated pace allowed ConEd to be operational and able to accommodate summer power demands in 2004.

The clear glass curtain wall is remarkable within its Manhattan context and was installed with exceptional efficiency. The reflector panel and overhanging glass at the spandrel condition provide a unique level of intricacy to the curtain wall, interacting and changing with the surrounding daylight and sky conditions. Simultaneously transparent and silvery opaque, the building's skin expresses a wide range of color, light, and reflection. From the interior, the full-height clear glass panels and transparent corners provide a unique sense of openness, as panoramic views extend from all angles.

The podium is clad in specially fabricated stainless steel screens embedded with motion-sensitive LEDs, as part of a collaboration between SOM and James Carpenter Design Associates. They were installed after the cable net entrance wall of the tenant lobby was completed.

The U.S. Green Building Council has certified the building at Gold status under its Leadership in Energy and Environmental Design (LEED) rating system, a first for a New York City office tower. It is being recognized for its pioneering approach to providing occupants wirth cleaner air and more natural light, while conserving energy and other natural resources.

Jenny Holzer's and James Carpenter's installation, *For 7 WTC*, chronicles New York through moving prose by poets, writers, and observers including Elizabeth Bishop, Allen Ginsberg, Langston Hughes, Walt Whitman, E. B. White, David Lehman, and others.

4

5

6

United States Census Bureau

Suitland, Maryland
Construction 2003–07

The United States Census Bureau won both a New York City Chapter AIA Honor Award and a 2002 GSA Design Excellence award, and the design has toured in exhibitions at the National Building Museum in Washington, DC, and the Center for Architecture in New York City.

Construction of the new headquarters, which is located in Suitland, Maryland, began in 2003, and is scheduled for completion in late 2007. Because the new buildings are being built around and between the Census Bureau's current facilities, construction has been phased to allow uninterrupted use. The curvilinear, fractured volumes of office space conform to existing structures and maximize daylight and views of the woodland preserve that envelops most of the ex-urban site. The soft, articulated forms of the buildings' cladding materials, which include landscaped roofs, latticed ivy walls, shaped, precast concrete, and laminated wood cladding systems recall the woods, and, when complete, will serve to minimize the visual impact of the new buildings on their surroundings.

1

2

3

1 Oblique view where exterior wall looks like one
  monolithic piece of wood

2 View looking up where each piece is recognizable

3 Interior view looking through wood outward

4 Wood blade pressure testing

5 Wood blade testing stability and waterproofing

Memorial Sloan-Kettering New Research Building

New York, New York
Construction 2003–06

Construction on the Memorial Sloan-Kettering New Research Building is well under way; Phase 1 completion is projected for the first quarter of 2006. Steel was topped out in June 2004. Currently, the building enclosure is close to completion, the majority of mechanical equipment is in place, and interior fit out has commenced on several lab floors and in the rectory. In-situ mockups of office and lab spaces have been built and viewed by MSK staff and administration. Four permanent art installations are being developed for public and common spaces throughout the building.

Upon completion of Phase 1, the adjacent 1950s-era lab building—located underneath the cantilevered southeast portion of the tower—will be decanted and demolished to make way for Phase 2 of the new facility.

1

2

3

1 South elevation

2 Laboratory enclosure with
ceramic frit pattern

3 Laboratory glazing viewed
from the interior

4 East elevation

4

5 Curtain wall in construction
6 North elevation in construction
7 South elevation
8 East elevation

7

8

Koch Center for Science, Mathematics, & Technology
Deerfield Academy

Deerfield, Massachusetts
Construction 2003–06

Construction of the Koch Center began in the fall of 2003. The building is scheduled for completion in summer 2006. A number of milestones were reached during the winter construction months. The steel structure for the building is highly complex due to the incorporation of numerous curvilinear forms in the design. Through careful coordination, the erection of the steel proceeded successfully. Construction crews are now nearing enclosure of the building. Ninety percent of the interior brick work is complete and the installation of skylights illuminating the brick is also virtually complete.

All of the LEED design components for the building are fully documented and the final package will be submitted shortly to the U.S. Green Building Council for analysis.

SOM hopes for a LEED Gold certification for the building. In anticipation of creating the infrastructure for the analemma projection in the principal commons space, a scale analemma mock-up was recently completed to verify all astronomical data required for the final installation.

2

3

1 View of south façade

2 View of trailing walls in
  surrounding landscape

3 View of path to entrance

4 View of entrance

4

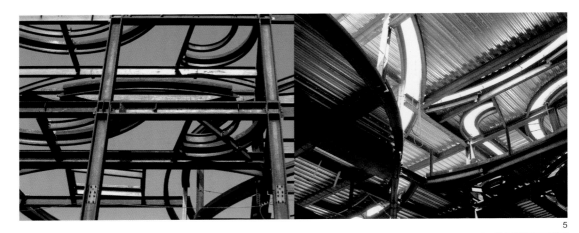

5

6

5 Detail views of steel frame

6 Detail of masonry façade

7 Interior view of science commons

7

Natalie de Blois Interviewed by Detlef Mertins

June 17, 2004
Chicago

Natalie de Blois was born in Paterson, New Jersey in 1921. She completed her professional degree in Architecture at Columbia University in 1944 and began a fifty-year career in architecture working initially with Ketchum, Gina & Sharp in New York. De Blois joined Skidmore, Owings and Merrill in September 1944 and worked as a designer with Gordon Bunshaft on many significant projects including Lever House, Pepsi Cola, Connecticut General Life Insurance, and Union Carbide, and as a designer for the Lever House. During this period she achieved national recognition for her designs. From 1962 to 1974 she worked in the Chicago offices of SOM where she became an associate partner in 1964. During the 1970s she became active in promoting greater awareness of women's issues within the profession and was celebrated as an outstanding figure in the field. From 1980 to 1993 she taught at the University of Texas at Austin, where a scholarship was created in her name. She became a Fellow of the American Institute of Architects in 1974 and in 1998 received the Romieniec Award of the Texas AIA for distinguished achievement in education.

Detlef Mertins is Professor and Chair of the Architecture Department at the University of Pennsylvania. He has written extensively on the history of modernism in the 20th century and has conducted interviews with former SOM partners Walter Netsch and Bruce Graham for SOM Journals 1 *and 2, and edited the interview with Gordon Bunshaft for* SOM Journal 3.

Detlef Mertens: What was it that drew you into architecture?

Natalie de Blois: My father was a civil engineer with a big family and I was brought up during the Depression. My parents wanted all their children to go to college, but they didn't have any money. They worked on getting us interested in going to college and expected that we all would. Mostly my father, but even my mother encouraged me as a young girl.

DM Specifically to study architecture?

NdB My father was an engineer, as were his father and grandfather. My mother was a schoolteacher. I was selected to be the one that would go into art. I told my father that I wanted to be an architect from the age of ten or twelve. He was always encouraging.

DM You went to Western College for Women in Oxford, Ohio, to begin with.

NdB I went there on a scholarship for one year only and then transferred to Columbia. My father wanted me to go to MIT. Of course, he didn't have any money. At that time you had to take two years of college to get into an architectural school. Columbia was still an undergraduate program.

So my father kept tabs on Columbia as an alternative. I had letters to the school and talked to them. They changed their rules that year to require only one year of college instead of two. It was during the War in 1940. The fact was that they wanted women. We had foreign and 4-F students in the program. It wasn't a large class. There were eighteen students including five women.

DM What was it like at Columbia?

133

Mario Salvadori, Natalie de Blois, and Philip Johnson in 1948

NdB I liked it. But already after my first year I thought, "Well, I want to get out of school and start working." But I didn't. I stayed. That was when I decided, "You're a woman and you're in a man's profession. You better get a degree." So I enjoyed my experience at Columbia. It was a good education. It wasn't a Beaux Arts school. We took a survey course in math, descriptive geometry, and statistics as well as an introduction to design and history. There were yearly courses in materials and methods of construction. And we always had painting and sculpture in the art school. Professor Lally was the structural engineer. He invented the Lally column, so who better than Professor Lally. We got an awful lot of background in technical subjects—in structures and mechanical engineering, and I was given an award for my ability to understand structures. It was a New York State exam award, and I got that for the school, for the graduating class.

DM Had you already started working at that time?

NdB Yes. During the War everybody had to work. We had to work to eat. The Navy was stationed at Columbia—they had classes there. I earned money by teaching drafting. At summer break I worked at Babcock & Wilcox,

who made boilers for the Russian Navy during the War. Their offices were in the Singer Sewing Machine Building in downtown New York. That was a great deal of fun. They wanted me to stay, and I vacillated but decided I'd go back to school.

During the school year, I worked for Frederick Kiesler. He was an architect and theater-set designer who taught at Columbia. He was able to draw well enough to get what he wanted built, like the chairs for Peggy Guggenheim's Art of This Century Gallery, but he didn't know how to finalize his drawings. So he hired me. He was a short little man and lived in an apartment house—a penthouse on 23rd and 10th or 11th Avenue. He had his penthouse scaled for himself. I remember being much impressed that the furniture was small. I worked in his apartment.

I don't think I ever saw the gallery finished, but I went up there with him in the service elevator. I remember one day as Mr. Kiesler walked me to the subway, he stopped and talked to somebody named Marcel Duchamp. He introduced me to him and afterwards said, "He's the man who painted *Nude Descending a Staircase.*"

DM How did you get from school to Skidmore?

NdB When I graduated in January 1944, I didn't have to look for a job. Morris Ketchum was a graduate of Columbia and he wanted to hire someone from my class, so I was chosen. Ketchum rented space from Wally Harrison in the International Building at Radio City. It was just a little room, about ten by fifteen feet. Ketchum had a desk at one end and Stanley Sharp and I were at the other end with the window.

Ketchum had done two spectacular modern shops on Fifth Avenue, Lederer's and Ciro's. They were some of the earliest modern architecture in New York City. So I was excited to work for Ketchum, because I knew he did modern architecture. I didn't want to do what we called eclectic architecture.

We worked every day, every night. We worked Saturday. We worked Sunday. We worked holidays—everything. We got $25 a week. That was good money.

It was a wonderful experience. Very intense. His office got bigger when he had enough work. He moved to a penthouse at 5 East 57th Street, which was where Skidmore was. I worked for Ketchum nine months. So it was probably after five or six months that we moved.

There was a fellow architect who joined the office. He used to take me out dancing to hear Benny Goodman and Tommy Dorsey. I went out with him quite often. He was very fond of me, but he was not encouraged. So he went to Mr. Ketchum and told him that he just couldn't work with me there. Mr. Ketchum called me over to his desk. We were all in one room. He said he was sorry, I'd have to leave. Just like that. Of course, I hadn't experienced a shock like that before.

DM You were just starting. You had been an excellent student, were doing good work, and suddenly . . .

NdB It all happened within a day. He said, "Well, I'll call up Mr. Skidmore. He's downstairs—see if he needs anybody." So he called up Skidmore and told me to go down there. There was no, "Sorry to see you go," or anything like that. Just "Pack up your things and move downstairs." So that's how I got to Skidmore.

I went down to Skidmore crushed, and was hired to do drafting on the Abraham Lincoln housing project. I worked just doing lettering and erasing and all those things. Of course, there was lots to learn.

Then before I knew it, Skidmore was asking me to work on design projects for him. There were no designers in those days.

DM Were you the first designer then?

NdB Well, I think I was. I was the first designer that the New York office had, other than the partners. In the beginning I worked on the bathhouses at Jones Beach. Of course, he got that because he had contacts with

Robert Moses. Skidmore was very much the society person. Always very nice, I thought. I knew his wife and met his children. Later he always talked to me about my family. When the Cincinnati Hotel job came in . . .

DM The Terrace Plaza Hotel.

NdB That was it.

Even before the Terrace Plaza we worked on the United Nations. Skidmore was a technical advisor to Wally Harrison on the UN headquarters. I was shipped down there for a while, and brought back to 5 East 57th Street to work on a renovation of the New York State Building from the 1939 World's Fair. In October 1946 the General Assembly meeting was held there. That was my design. I was on the front page of *The New York Herald Tribune*. This is how exciting it was. I worked on the renovation and the translations booth and the dais. I did a lot of drawing, and studies of alternatives. You realize there are millions of solutions.

For the Terrace Plaza, it was a mixed-use building, which is interesting for that time. Thomas Emery Sons owned the Netherlands Plaza Hotel in Cincinnati. They purchased a nearby half-block and made long-term leases with two department stores, J.C. Penney and Bond's Men's Clothing. The hotel was built above these. I was never sent to Cincinnati.

DM This is a project where you did everything. You did the planning, designed the structure and the interiors.

NdB The scheme of the two commercial buildings and the hotel was worked out with the client. The sketches

New York Herald Tribune, October 24, 1946

Terrace Plaza Hotel, 1948

Terrace Plaza Hotel Restaurant with Miró mural

are all by me. I did the works. Skidmore said they'd never done a hotel, and that's true. The Oak Ridge project in Tennessee gave the firm credibility. It was a very secret project.

When it came time to locate a small dining room on the top of the building, I came up with six or eight different schemes. Mr. Skidmore took them all down to Cincinnati and they decided they liked the one with the circular plan. Mr. Skidmore called me up and said, "Natalie, they like the round one. Go ahead . . ."

DM Was it your favorite too?

NdB No, it wasn't my favorite. Mine was rectangular. It wasn't cantilevered like that. It really went out like the rest of the building.

John Emery was the head of the Cincinnati Museum of Art and he hired Miró to do a mural in that room. Miró came to New York and painted it up in Harlem. I went to see it. It was in a great, big, open kind of space, maybe a garage. Before sending it to Cincinnati, they exhibited it at the Museum of Modern Art. This was in 1950. They put my rendering of the space next to Miró's painting. Here I was in the Museum of Modern Art and there was an article about it in *The New York Herald Tribune:* "Miro Has Fun Painting Cincinnati Mural." It includes the picture. I imagine Skidmore's name was on it, but my

name wasn't. I designed it all, did the planning and the sections and the elevations, and it was published all over.

DM When Gordon [Bunshaft] came into the office after the War, did you start working with him right away?

NdB No, we were still working on the hotel. Gordon was very interested in the art program—the Steinberg mural in the dining room and the Stuart Davis sculpture in the bar, the Miró mural, and the Calder in the lobby.

DM Was the art program for the hotel Emery's idea?

NdB Emery hired Miró. I don't think Skidmore would have gone out and hired Miró or even have suggested it. Certainly Bill Brown wouldn't have. So I'm sure that Emery started it, and then Skidmore hired Ben Baldwin, an architect, to work on some of the interiors. He worked on the bar. I worked on the lounge, cafeteria, and the hotel rooms—everything else.

You asked about Gordon, I remember he introduced me to Sandy Calder and we went out to lunch. He used Calder on many other buildings too that I worked on. I was busy when he came into the office, and he started working on the Veterans Hospital in Brooklyn. I didn't work on that.

DM What was the first project the two of you worked on?

NdB It was the New York University Medical Center.

Miro Has Fun Painting Cincinnati Mural

Combines Bright Colors and Nonsense in Panel for Hotel Penthouse

THE fun-loving Rover boy of modern painting, Joan Miro, has just produced his first mural, and probably his first important painting—a 32-foot guache that will hang on the curved wall of a glass penthouse atop Cincinnati's new Terrace Plaza Hotel. The mural has been temporarily but sympathetically installed at the Museum of Modern Art.

The $12,000,000 Cincinnati hotel, designed by the New York architects Skidmore, Owings, and Merrill for Thomas Emery's Sons, Inc., will be open for business this summer. The twelve stories of the hotel on top of a seven-story business structure make a total of nineteen stories to tower over Cincinnati's other buildings. The glass (Continued on page 3, cols. an 7)

Artist's sketch of the roof-top dining penthouse of the Terrace Plaza Hotel in Cincinnati, at top, and close-up of a section of Joan Miro's fanciful, thirty-two-foot guache mural in the room

New York Herald Tribune, March 7, 1948

DM The hospital was in the 1950 MoMA show as a project.

NdB Yes. We worked initially on the rehabilitation building. After the war, rehabilitation was a big thing. Then I worked with Gordon on the alumni center and the other elements of the complex.

DM The photograph of the model is interesting because it shows how it fit into the city around it.

NdB Yes. The project included a school, a library and dormitories, doctors' offices, and a hospital.

DM Did you do the programming for it?

NdB No, Bob Cutler had a staff who did the program. Roy Schmauder did hospital programming, which became very specialized. He also did laboratory programming.

DM In this project, like the hotel, every piece of the program is given its own expression and then combined into an ensemble. It's an enormous project, so this design strategy seems to work well. It lets you develop or change a part without affecting the whole.

NdB The big overall project was developed so that they could go out and raise money. I'm not sure that I even worked on it later. There were so many projects coming up, one right after the other.

DM Did you see the exhibition at MoMA?

NdB Yes, I did. The first thing you saw was the model of Lever House. It was small but spectacular. I hadn't seen the model before. Of course, this is 1950, so there were lots of hospitals and schools and shopping centers. I designed shopping centers. Then Gordon and I did some work for the First National Bank in Fort Worth, Texas.

DM Gordon called you his best designer when he introduced you to his clients.

NdB Yes.

DM What was it about your work that he liked?

NdB He often liked my ideas and I understood what he wanted.

DM Were your sensibilities closely attuned?

NdB I wouldn't quite say that. I always thought it was wonderful that Gordon was a modernist. Most of the architects in New York weren't doing modern architecture at that time.

DM Did you clash?

New York University Medical Center, 1945

137

NdB No, we didn't clash. We never clashed. He would do things that were strange, perhaps.

We had a big meeting about the Kennedy International Airport job. Calder was doing a big mobile in it. We had a presentation board that was enormous, in several pieces. We were getting ready for that meeting. Gordon looked at me and he said, "You can't come to the meeting unless you go home first and change your clothes. I don't like green." So I went home and changed my clothes and then went to the meeting.

DM Did he ever say that to a man?

NdB No, of course not. These were things that had to do with being female, I guess. Another time a mock-up was made in Westchester, which is north of New York City. He said, "Meet me Saturday at such-and-such an hour," because he wanted to look at the mockup, and he wanted me to be there so I would know what he wanted. So I drove from Connecticut on a Saturday. I had three or four children in the back seat of my car. We went to the mockup site. Gordon was there with Nina, his wife, and their dog. He had the dog running in an outside area. He said, "Don't bring your kids in here Natalie. They can't come in here because the dog is here." I had to leave my children out in the car in the parking lot.

But he was supportive too. I applied for a Fulbright in 1950 when I was working on the Istanbul Hilton Hotel. I thought, "Wouldn't this be great." I had one child at that time. Gordon wrote glowing letters. I had to include pictures of what I was working on. He said, "Tell them you designed it all." He was very supportive of me in this fashion, professionally. But his treatment of me as a woman was typical of that time.

When I was working on Connecticut General, I was pregnant with my third son. I was invited to the opening and he said, "You know, don't come to the opening if you haven't had that baby yet." I had four children between 1948 and 1957, which was when all these buildings were done. I went to the hospital from the office and then I came back to the office a week after that. No maternity leave. With the first child I did take time because I was sick. At Christmas when the bonuses were given out, I was told I had only worked from the time I had had the baby. I remember complaining to the man who did the finances. I said, "I started work in 1944, not in 1948."

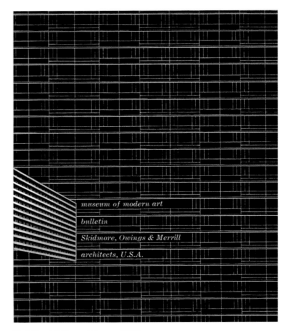

museum of modern art
bulletin
Skidmore, Owings & Merrill
architects, U.S.A.

MoMA exhibition catalogue, 1950

Louis Skidmore with Lever House Model, MoMA exhibition, 1950

Because I was out for two or three months, he had started the count all over again.

DM Let's talk a bit about Connecticut General. How did you come to the idea that you would make a single mass instead of composing with different building masses— just one very, very large floor plan with courtyards in it. That seems like a new idea at that point.

NdB I came back from Germany in 1953, after I was on the Fulbright, and the programming for Connecticut General had just been finished by Roger Radford. Roger came up with alternate schemes—a high-rise building, a low-rise building, and multi-buildings. I never saw these alternatives. The client selected the low-rise scheme. Then I diagrammed and assigned areas. The courtyards were located in this low-rise scheme so that no employee had a workstation more than thirty feet from a window. Roger was put on another project. I worked the whole time on the building after that. It was the first job where we worked with Isamu Noguchi.

DM It's interesting that the building is lifted up off the ground creating an expansive and open ground plane with landscaped courtyards. Were you thinking of this as a public space? Other projects also have this kind of public ground plane.

NdB Many Skidmore projects had open public ground planes inspired by Mies van der Rohe or Le Corbusier. But at Connecticut General the ground floor was not thought to be public space, since it had other functions like employee recreation and services, dining, and a large computer facility.

With the Düsseldorf Consulate, we had a good excuse for lifting the building off the ground. That was security. In fact, we were ahead of the game in terms of security. The outdoor terrace was designed by Noguchi, who I worked with on the Lever House and Emhart projects. Gordon didn't like one of the four courts designed by Noguchi. He showed me what Noguchi had done and said, "Now Natalie you design this one." So I designed the fourth one.

DM These are great buildings. I wanted to also ask you about the Hilton Hotel in Istanbul which you worked on. There are a number of buildings from the 1950s that have a grid-like façade. The building appears like a cage.

NdB This building was a concrete box frame. I did research, and decided that's the way it should be done.

Connecticut General Life Insurance, north wing, 1954–57

Connecticut General Life Insurance, view from south, 1954–57

When we did Terrace Plaza Hotel, we had beams between rooms or between every other room at thirty-foot intervals. I thought, "We have to get rid of these dropped beams." I had seen some other hotels with box frames in publications. It's good acoustically and structurally. I said that that's what I wanted to do, and Gordon said, "Sure."

DM How did you feel about the fluid relationship that you had to many projects—that you might come and go on a project and others did too? Was that kind of teamwork satisfying?

NdB I never had any problems. To begin with, on some of the buildings, other people did the programming. Or people were already on it, but you worked with them.

DM It seems generous for work to be shared that way, and that various people can make contributions according to their own strengths and interests, but then it's a collective project.

NdB Oh, it is a collective project. In the beginning of the job, we would sit around and talk about the materials, the degree of finish and the cost. I counted on civil and mechanical engineers. Some of my best experiences were working with someone like Mr. Weiskopf who died years and years ago. Because basically I'm interested in the nuts and bolts of how you put things together. In Chicago they didn't quite understand what I wanted.

DM How did you get along with them if you wanted to have more involvement in the nuts and bolts? What happened during the construction stage?

NdB Shop drawings and site supervision were important. A lot of these projects, like Connecticut General, were done with people I worked with over and over again.

DM You got to know each other really well.

NdB Yes, for sure. New York was different than Chicago. Chicago had mechanical and structural engineers in the office. In New York, we were in a small office and went out for the engineers.

DM You also did Pepsi Cola, which is an extraordinary essay in lightness and transparency—crisp, orthogonal, almost levitating. Is that the kind of architecture you preferred?

NdB Yes, I loved doing it. Bob Cutler was the project manager. He was a friend of the president.

DM What were you trying to achieve at Pepsi Cola?

Hilton Hotel Istanbul, 1955

Hilton Hotel Istanbul, penthouse, 1955

NdB Gordon asked me, "What can we do there," and so I did the zoning and massing studies of the building. I had come up with the zoning. There were no alternatives. The zoning was affected by the small site and the height of the adjacent buildings. Gordon came up with the structural concept so that there were no columns on the exterior walls. It was a smooth box.

When we first started on it, we worked on the site as though it included five extra pieces of property along 58th Street that were later built into an apartment house by James Polshek. Pepsi-Cola couldn't acquire them. So we went ahead with the small site. It could have come out further along 59th Street, but then it would have had to step back. Gordon decided against that.

DM How did you decide that the ground plan should be so open—that the building should appear to be levitating?

NdB That was what we all liked and what we did often.

DM How did the design of the curtain wall come about?

NdB The curtain wall is in twelve-foot modules. Not five feet, not six feet, but twelve feet. You can't do twelve-foot modules and give a client flexibility with the layout of offices. Once we found out how big the building was and how many twelve-foot offices we could put in, we came up with a scheme for movable mullions so that you could have fifteen-foot offices, or nine-foot offices without breaking up the exterior. I felt it was interesting that Gordon was going to impose that on this client. I think it was a good idea for this client. He wasn't really that concerned about the offices. The columns were set back along 59th Street to accommodate secretarial space. We made the glass just about as big as you could make it at that time. We always did custom window walls, because if you're doing a whole building, there is no point in using stock elements. I think General Bronze did the window wall fabrication.

DM Tell me about the time you were on television.

NdB Around 1960, I was selected to be the lead person on the television show "To Tell the Truth." I was on stage with several other women and we were asked by Dorothy Kilgalin and Don Ameche, and others to guess which one of us was the woman who designed the recent 103-story Union Carbide Building. A couple of them guessed correctly, and a couple of them didn't. The

Pepsi Cola Company Headquarters, entrance view, 1958–59

Union Carbide Corporation, 1957–60

next day, Mr. Owens called me from California. He had heard I was on TV. He asked, "Why didn't you tell me you were going to be on TV?" so he could have seen it. His taxi driver in San Francisco said he had just seen somebody from Skidmore Owings and Merrill on TV. All kinds of people—the man who was in charge of Connecticut General had seen it and wrote me a letter.

DM That would have been about the same time as the article on SOM in *Fortune* magazine that included you.

NdB Yes, it was.

DM It's interesting that in the late 1950s your work was publicly recognized. You were closely identified with specific buildings.

NdB Yes, I had a lot of publicity. Later, when I was living in Austin, Texas, one of my neighbors went on a guided tour of New York City, where they pointed out this building [Union Carbide] and said it was designed by a woman architect, Natalie de Blois. She came back and couldn't believe that she was living in the neighborhood with somebody who had designed that building in New York. So I was always given a lot of the credit for that as the project designer.

DM What were the big challenges for you on the Union Carbide tower?

NdB It was on the railroad tracks, so we had problems with where to put the mechanical and electrical services. You couldn't put them in the basement. We had a little bit of a basement on Madison Avenue. But it couldn't have served this building because there was no way of getting across the tracks. So that was a challenge.

DM Did you do the zoning on that project?

NdB Yes, I did. Gordon wanted the building to go straight up. Based on that, we determined where the columns had to be. So that was very interesting. Then we did a lot of detailed studies about materials and the lighting system inside and out.

DM The photograph of the office interiors with the luminous ceiling has become an icon of the period.

NdB We integrated the air diffusers and lights with the partitions. We had to have it all tested. You don't get a chance to design the light fixtures in most buildings. It was that big a building. You don't see any grills for the air. That was very special.

DM Did you make a full-scale mockup of the interiors as you did on other projects?

NdB We always did mockups. The design had to be tested, technically and visually.

DM Would you describe the team of people working with you?

NdB It was a good-sized team. We had people working on partition systems and air conditioning. We had structural and mechanical engineers.

DM But before you got to the construction drawings . . .

NdB Structural and mechanical requirements influenced design development, especially on this project. I often had a team who worked for me all the time. They would go from one job to another.

DM That would give you a lot of consistency. You often worked with the same job captain and with Gordon as

F O R T U N E

William S. Brown of the New York office is partner-in-charge of the Union Carbide project. He has presided over teams that produced some of S.O.M.'s most brilliant results in office buildings: e.g., Lever House, Connecticut General.

Natalie de Blois, senior designer, did the preliminary drawings of the Union Carbide tower and plaza, now oversees the five junior designers who are working out the details. This is the first skyscraper that Mrs. de Blois has designed.

Fortune Magazine, January 1958, "Architects from Skid's Row"

the partner. You had your own staff. Even though a lot of people moved around within the firm, there was also a lot of continuity. The team was able to move from one project to another.

NdB Moving around happens because clients can't make up their minds, or change their minds. The project stops for a while or you wait for decisions. Given all the projects that other people were working on, you had to be prepared to move around, back and forth.

DM What were the circumstances that led you to leave New York?

NdB After I had my fourth child, I divorced my husband. He remarried and moved to Chicago. His second wife wrote that she'd like to help take care of the children. So in the summer of 1962 I brought the two younger boys

out to Chicago. I wanted to take the two older boys to Greece and Turkey. That was the first time I saw the hotel in Istanbul. That was when I walked into the Skidmore office in Chicago.

DM What did you think when Bruce Graham asked you to come and work with him?

NdB I said I would think about it, and I spoke to Gordon. Gordon told me three things. He said, "You can go out to Chicago if you want. If you go, you must realize that you'll never be a partner." I wasn't aiming to be a partner. I was perfectly happy doing what I was doing. There was an article published that had said, "Isn't that funny she's never become a partner." That's maybe how that idea started.

Secondly, he said I'd never get along with Bruce, and thirdly, I could always come back. Then I had to make up my mind. There were other reasons for going too. New York was comparatively slow then.

DM What was your first building in Chicago?

NdB Equitable Life Assurance was the first. The concept had already been developed and the project was under contract. But there was still a lot of work to do. At first in Chicago, I worked with Bruce on Horizon House, a Tishman construction project. I first worked with developers on the Emhart project.

DM That was in the 1960s when the development industry really began to take shape. Was it better than working for clients who would occupy the buildings?

NdB No, not better, but certainly different. They had different aims. One was trying to make money, and the other was trying to satisfy their client.

DM Did the developers take over a lot of decision-making from the architects?

NdB Oh yes. There is no question about that.

DM Why do you say then that it was good to work with them?

NdB Because you learned a lot.

DM What did you learn?

NdB You learn how much things cost and about new technology. They had new ideas. It was good fun. They were so quick. Materials and methods of construction were changing and the developers were sharp. And you knew where you stood.

DM Did you make decisions quickly?

NdB Yes.

DM Did you always know what you wanted?

NdB Not always.

DM In the Chicago office, did you get credit for your work?

NdB Bruce never gave me any credit.

DM Was it a policy not to give credit to team members?

NdB No, it was not.

DM Hadn't he asked you to come there?

NdB Yes, he did ask me and he did make me an associate partner in 1964.

DM When did you realize he was not happy with your work?

NdB He made me aware of the fact on several different occasions when I was working on the World Bank in Washington and later the Boots Pure Drug Company in Nottingham, England.

DM But it was not the kind of relationship that you had with Gordon.

NdB No. It was an entirely different relationship.

DM Did he discriminate against you as a woman?

NdB No, I don't think so. He discriminated against me because he was perhaps insecure. According to Jack Train, who used to work at Skidmore, Bruce hired me because he wanted to say, "Hey look what I did. I brought Natalie to Chicago." Bruce went through designers quickly. He didn't keep designers around very long.

DM What happened when he stopped wanting to work with you?

NdB He gave me uninteresting small projects. He didn't tell me what the problem was. He didn't speak to me. He went to Fred Kraft who was a managing partner. He told Fred he wanted to get rid of me. Fred, who was a good friend of mine, told me this. Bruce had called up Gordon and Gordon said, "You can't get rid of her." I could go back to New York, but I still had three sons in school in Chicago. So the office came up with the solution that Myron [Goldsmith] would take me. I thought Myron was a dear, sweet fellow, but he couldn't make up his mind. He didn't know what he wanted. I worked with him on several projects, including the St. Joseph Valley Bank in Elkhart, Indiana Bank. I worked on it with the client and I went to all the meetings, designed the inside of the building. In his book, Myron lists everybody scrupulously but he never mentioned me.

DM For that project or in the whole book?

Equitable Life Assurance, 1965

NdB In the whole book. I used to think he was a nice person. I don't think that anymore.

DM Is it true that you were excluded from lunch meetings at men's clubs?

NdB That happened at partners meetings. It happened in New York from the very beginning at the Metropolitan Club and it happened in Chicago.

DM No women were allowed into those buildings I assume.

NdB Yes. The first time I was working on the Terrace Plaza Hotel a meeting of all the food service people was being held. Walt Severinghaus was in charge of the meeting. When it was time to break for lunch he said, "Natalie, please be back here at two o'clock. We're going out to lunch." This upset me, but I didn't think of it as segregation.

DM In New York or when you moved to Chicago?

NdB Chicago. It always upset me. I can't remember Gordon ever saying "Natalie, you can't eat with us."

DM How did you get involved with women's organizations in the early 1970s?

NdB In 1973 I was one of the founding members of the "Chicago Women in Architecture." When we first started those meetings, for two or three years, we were going strong. We had a group of about ten loyal women, including Carol Barney and Margaret Young. I thought it was an issue of getting together with like women and supporting them in whatever way we could. Consciousness-raising was just a little bit over my head. I didn't go for that. In 1973, I was invited to Washington University. One of our members had gone to Washington University in St. Louis. They planned to have a "Women and Minorities" conference and this woman asked me if I'd speak.

DM You gave two papers, I believe.

NdB Yes. That was the first time I went to this sort of meeting. And I was just amazed! There were all these people out there, men and women, asking questions and, saying "How did you do this?" and "How did you do that?"

DM You were just on the verge of leaving the firm. You left the next year.

NdB Yes, in 1974, after thirty years. At the "Women and Minorities" conference I ran into my friend Judy Edelman, who had gone to Columbia and was in the class behind me. Judy was involved in the National Women in Architecture Task Force of the American Institute of Architects, which had been started. She asked me to take Joan Sprague's place in 1975. So I went to Washington and took part in the task force. The task force had specific aims and goals that concerned women in the profession.

Between 1973 and 1975 I also attended several conferences put on by the Association of Collegiate Schools of Architecture. I took part in some reviews at Chicago Circle Campus and decided I would like to teach. While I was still in Chicago, I also went to New York to talk with Susana Torre and Judith Paine who were writing a book and planning an exhibition at the Brooklyn Museum called *Women in Architecture*. It traveled around the U.S. and was very influential. The show came to Houston when I was there, and I took part in making that possible.

DM What did you do when you left SOM?

NdB I took a long vacation and rode my bicycle around France and Germany. And I traveled through England. I had always had three weeks vacation. After I moved to Chicago, I used to take my children to Europe in those weeks. We traveled in small areas.

DM Were your children with you in 1974 too?

NdB No. I went by myself, and then joined my oldest son who was studying in Tübingen, Gemany.

DM At that point they must have been grown up. Raising four children through all this was an extraordinary accomplishment. Were the people in the office aware of the fact that you had four children and that you were responsible for your family as well as your work?

NdB A few did who I knew quite well. But I didn't have pictures of my children on my desk.

DM How did your children feel about you being a professional woman spending so much time working?

NdB You'd have to ask them. They are very supportive and proud of their mother.

DM What did you do after leaving SOM and after your bicycle trip to Europe?

NdB I had to work. At that time there were quite a few people leaving SOM. The office was trimming down. There wasn't a lot of work. Work was slow in New York too. So I went to Houston because that is where there was a lot of work. There were about six or eight Skidmore people in the office of Neuhaus and Taylor, later called 3-D International. They asked me if I would come down. So I went to Houston for an interview. I had never looked for a job before. Ketchum had come to me and then Skidmore was given to me.

So I took the SOM book to an interview in Houston. Of course, they loved it and they hired me. They did a lot of overseas work. I went to Riyadh and designed the Pan-American Hotel, which was never built. That was fun. I enjoyed that. But every single year there was a different partner in charge of design. People got fired. People got hired. People left. Harwood Taylor, who had hired me, committed suicide. So after four years, I left. My youngest son had started engineering school at the University of

Texas, so I went to Austin. Austin is a nice city. We got on our bikes and kept going and going. I liked that. So I came back again and bought a house.

I bought the house from a real estate agent in Austin whose husband was the Dean of the architecture school there—Hal Box. The agent went home and told her husband that she had sold a house to a woman architect. He said, "Who?" She said, "Natalie De Blois." I had met him at conference of the Association of Collegiate Schools of Architecture at Cranbrook. He called me up and asked me to teach at the school. I could teach when I wanted, as long as I wanted, and whatever I wanted.

DM What an offer!

NdB I started out by teaching part-time. I just loved to teach. I loved the students. I had such a wonderful time. It was also very educational for me because I no longer could count on structural engineers and civil engineers, and people at my beck and call to answer all my questions. I had to teach everything.

When I went down there, Hal Box said he didn't think that the students would like doing high-rise buildings. But the students loved doing high-rise buildings. They came to the class once and they wanted to take it the next year and the next. I had some students who were able to wrangle themselves into my class three years running. They just thought it was the best thing in the world.

This was Texas. They didn't know anything about elevators. The teachers did houses. So they used to say, "Come teach my students how to design an office building." I enjoyed it. After I had been there maybe five or six years, I found out that if I stayed for ten years, I could get retirement pay. So I stayed thirteen years. I quit when I was seventy-three. I could have stayed. At the time, I was also working as a consultant for a fellow named David Graeber, who had been one of the four people in charge of design at 3-D International. That's where I met him. He was just a great friend and a very exciting person to work for. His spirit and his interest in what I was doing was great. So he hired me as a consultant on several jobs while I was teaching part-time.

DM You stopped teaching in 1993, which is really not that long ago. It's a little over ten years now. Are you still in touch with any of the students?

NdB Oh lots of them. That's a wonderful thing. They call me when they open up their offices, or get married. There's a picture of me with four former students seventeen years ago in the New York office of SOM. The former UT students were all working at Skidmore. You see, they wanted to go and work at Skidmore too.

Natalie de Blois (fourth from left) with former students in 1988 at the New York offices of SOM

The courtyard in the Lever Brothers Company Headquarters

Lincoln Center Library, 1965

Hilton Hotel, Istanbul, 1955

Timeline of Projects

Natalie de Blois
1943–74

*Worked as senior designer
List prepared by Nicholas Adams in consultation with Natalie de Blois, March 2005

1943–47
Partners Louis Skidmore and William S. Brown

New York Housing Authority, Abraham Lincoln House; New York, NY; draftsperson

Long Island State Park Commission, comfort stations and beach facilities; Jones Beach, NY; design studies

Renovation of the New York State Building in Flushing Meadows for the first United Nations, General Assembly; New York, NY; design drawings.

Thomas Emery's Sons Inc., Terrace Plaza Hotel; Cincinnati, OH; overall design responsibilities

1948–51
Design partner Gordon Bunshaft

New York University Medical Center, Bellevue Medical Center, master plan with detailed studies for Institute for Rehabilitation, Residence Hall, and Alumni Center; New York, NY*

Greenwich Hospital Association, 300-bed general hospital; Greenwich, CT*

Ford Motor Company, Ford Properties, master plan with two office buildings, low-rise garage, service complex; Dearborn, MI; responsible for low-rise facilities*

Owens-Corning Fiberglas Corporation, office and display room; New York, NY

Hilton Hotel, 300-room hotel; Istanbul, Turkey*

Lever Brothers Company, headquarters office building, worked directly with Bunshaft on design of plaza, lobby, cafeteria, and first three floors; New York, NY

Creole Petroleum, town plan for 20,000 employees; Amuay Bay, Venezuela

Massachusetts Institute of Technology, Karl Taylor Compton Laboratories; Cambridge, MA

Borden Company, processing plant, Bainbridge, NY

Grout Park Elementary School; Schenectady, NY

Community Hospital; Gouverneur, NY

Alexandra Bay, Edward John Noble Hospital, 30-bed hospital; New York, NY

1952–61
Design partner Gordon Bunshaft, after the Fullbright Fellowship Prize, 1952. Made participating associate in 1954

United States Government, State Department, Foreign Buildings Operations, Consular-Amerikahaus, three consulates, and two apartment houses; Bremen, Dusseldorf, and Stuttgart, Germany*

Connecticut General Life Insurance Company, office building; Bloomfield, CT*

Great Southern Life Insurance Company, office building; Houston, TX*

Girl Scouts of the United States of America, office building; New York, NY*

Ciba-Geigy Corporation, research laboratories and office buildings; Ardsley, NY

World's Fair, master plan proposal; New York, NY; terminated before completion*

Pepsico Inc., headquarters office building including interiors; New York, NY*

Yale University, computer center; New Haven, CT*

Harry A. Conte Elementary School and Community Center; New Haven, CT*

Union Carbide Corporation, headquarters office building including interiors; New York, NY*

Lincoln Center for the Performing Arts, Library and Museum for the Performing Arts (building design and coordination with adjacent Vivian Beaumont Theater); New York, NY*

Emhart Corporation, administration and research building; Bloomfield, CT*

1952–61
Buildings undertaken with other designers

First National Bank, bank and office building; Fort Worth, TX

Kennedy International Airport, International Arrival and Airlines Building expansion; New York, NY

Arabian-American Oil Company, office building; Dahrain, Saudi Arabia

1962–68
Design partner Bruce Graham. Made associate partner in 1964

Equitable Life Assurance, office building; Chicago, IL*

Horizon House Apartment Buildings, 520 units in two towers, Tishman Realty; Fort Lee, NJ*

Sunbeam Electronics, engineering and manufacturing facility; Fort Lauderdale, FL*

Boots Pure Drug Company, headquarters office building and interiors; Nottingham, England*

Hartford Fire Insurance Company, office building; Hartford, CT*

International Bank for Reconstruction and Development, World Bank, headquarters office building; Washington, DC*

Bond Court, office building and garage (Miller-Tishman Venture); Cleveland, OH*

Dow Chemical Company, Site Development Design Guidelines including landscape, lighting, parking lots, architectural elements and graphics for 1,800-acre site report; Freeland, MI*

1969–74
Design partner Myron Goldsmith

Arthur Anderson & Company, Training Center for Professional Development, classrooms, dormitory and auditorium; Elgin, IL*

St. Joseph Valley Bank, headquarters bank and office building and interiors; Elkhart, IN*

Oliver-Tyrone Corporation, Diamond Shamrock, office building with commercial and parking facilities; Cleveland, OH*

Oliver-Tyrone Corporation, Equibank, office building, bank, and garage; Pittsburgh, PA*

Department of Public Works, O'Hare, Jefferson Park study for Park & Ride; Chicago, IL*

Associates Corporation, study of prototype commercial building; South Bend, IN*

John Merrill, Nathanial Owings, and Louis Skidmore (from left), in 1953

Essays

Three's Company : The Early Years of Skidmore & Owings

Nicholas Adams

Nicholas Adams is the Mary Conover Mellon professor in the history of architecture at Vassar College, Poughkeepsie, NY. He is the author of Skidmore, Owings & Merrill: The Experiment Since 1936, *published by Electa (Milan), May 2006. He has been editor of the* Journal of the Society of Architectural Historians *and currently serves on the editorial board of* Casabella. *He has been a fellow of the American Academy in Rome and the Institute for Advanced Study in Princeton, NJ. Most recently he has been working on a book on the Swedish architect Gunnar Asplund and his Law Court extension in Gothenburg.*

Counterfactuals are a form of historical enquiry much in vogue. Is it no more than a parlor game to ask what would the world have looked like had the Soviets not seized power in Russia? Had the Chinese authorities not suppressed the student revolts in Tiananmen Square? Had an arrow not pierced the eye of Harald at the Battle of Hastings in 1066? Or is there something deeper to be learned, from both the answer and the question.[1] Much of the recent debate about controlling Saddam Hussein in the period prior to the beginning of the invasion of Iraq was based on counterfactual arguments concerning the so-called Munich Pact between Hitler and Chamberlain in 1939. Had Hitler been stopped in Czechoslovakia, might we have avoided World War II? Counterfactuals are not neutral investigative tools, but they can force us to examine the assumptions that rest behind the way things are, inducing us to think more deeply about what forces and influences made events turn out the way they did.

Architecture is a field ripe for the counterfactual. Every architectural competition contains implicit possibilities about the shape of the field. What would have happened if Eliel Saarinen's entry had been picked for the Chicago Tribune? And, if thereafter, Alvar Aalto decided to stay on in the United States in 1939 (or 1949) instead of returning to Finland? And what if, instead of opening a new office in New York in 1937, Louis Skidmore had taken the job as head of architecture at the Armour Institute, in Chicago, that he had been offered? Imagine a strong Scandinavian presence in North America and no opening for Mies van der Rohe in Chicago! Counterfactuals can boil over quickly into fantasy. In this brief article I want to bring forward a counterfactual that is part of the history of SOM. What would the firm look like today if in the moments after its birth, it had kept a fourth partner on its masthead?

Louis Skidmore and Nathaniel Owings formed their partnership, "Skidmore & Owings," on January 1, 1936, in Chicago. Shortly thereafter they opened an office in New York City, a result of a commission to provide a product display exhibition for American Standard in Raymond Hood's Radiator Building, New York. Louis Skidmore became head of the office in New York and he soon hired the nucleus of the firm: Robert W. Cutler, William S. Brown, J. Walter Severinghaus, and Gordon Bunshaft. Owings, in Chicago, was a little less successful. At the beginning there was no one in Chicago to handle design with the skill of Bunshaft, and when important commissions came up there, he flew out to oversee Owings' team. The other notable lack in the young firm, then with no more than thirty employees in both New York and Chicago, was an engineer-partner. All this changed in 1939–40, when the firm was barely three years old. Two men were hired, both of whom were given partnerships and placed on the masthead of the firm. One of these hires (in 1939) is well known: his name was John Ogden Merrill (1896–1975). Merrill had been a drinking buddy of Skidmore and Owings, who had lost his job when the two senior partners in the firm where he was working died.[2]

The American Standard Exhibition, New York, 1938. This commission triggered the opening of the New York SOM office.

Merrill had trained at the University of Wisconsin in civil engineering (1914–17) and then at MIT in architecture (1919–21), like Skidmore and Bunshaft, and he was an important person within the Chicago architectural community serving as president of the local chapter of the American Institute of Architects (1935–37). His official position for Skidmore & Owings was partner in charge of engineering and there was some hope, given his experience with federal housing, that he would help the firm find commissions in that area, as well as provide expertise in engineering.[3]

In 1940, Skidmore and Owings made another appointment, this time for the New York office: W. Earle Andrews (1899–1965) thus making the firm Skidmore Owings Merrill & Andrews. But who was Andrews? What was the idea behind his appointment? Why do we know nothing about him? And what would it have meant had "SOM" been "SOMA"?

William Earle Andrews was born in Hampton, Virginia and studied (without receiving a degree) at the College of William & Mary. He served his apprenticeship as a draftsman with M. P. Andrews & Company (possibly a firm owned by a relative) and then went to work as a draftsman, surveyor, and inspector for the Virginia State Highway Commission (1921–22; 1924); an engineer for the Sam L. Matz Coal Corporation (1922–24); and as an engineer and superintendent at M. T. McArthur Construction (1925–27).[4] In 1927 he took up a special series of appointments: as deputy chief engineer to the Long Island State Parks Commission; he was in charge of design and construction for the Long Island State Parks and Parkways including Jones Beach.[5] Later, he became chief engineer and general superintendent for the New York City Parks Department, and chief engineer (and from 1934 general manager) for the Henry Hudson Parkway Authority and the Marine Parkway Authority.[6] His employer was Robert Moses, and Andrews was one of Moses' closest associates.

No description of the American city today should ever fail to mention Robert Moses (1888–1981). A builder of highways, bridges, and parks, his influence, even half a century after he was at the peak of his power, is still felt almost daily by every resident in New York City and in many other American cities. He was, as his biographer Robert A. Caro called him, the great expert in the "art of

Robert Moses in 1938

Park Expert Seeks Sites For Boy Scouts' Camps

W. Earle Andrews

W. Earle Andrews, engineer expert on park and recreational projects and consulting engineer for the World's Fair, will direct a survey designed to increase the outdoor facilities available for New York City boys, it was announced yesterday by the Boy Scout Federation of Greater New York.

The survey, it was announced, is the first step in a program of camp expansion, in which sites will be sought near the city. Outdoor activities are planned for the camps during the Summer and throughout the rest of the year on week-ends and holidays.

W. Earle Andrews, in *The New York Times,* November 21, 1938

Getting Things Done in a democratic society."[7] Andrews helped him in his great mission: building the bridges around New York. And with the tolls he collected from the bridges, he built the highways, and then built recreation areas to which people would travel over his roads and bridges. Although an unelected political appointee, Moses had power in New York City that was virtually unassailable for forty years. Andrews was, "Moses' right hand man" (*New York Times,* May 5, 1934) representing Moses at meetings, carrying on business when the boss was away, and serving him faithfully for many years. He

The Westinghouse Electric & Manufacturing Company, NY World's Fair in 1939, one of a number of SOM projects there.

even knew one of Moses' darkest secrets, the existence of his destitute brother Paul Moses, whom Andrews employed in 1962 as an errand "boy" at $96.16 a week.[8] Moses was Louis Skidmore's friend, too.[9] Moses placed him on the Long Island State Park Commission Board and helped Skidmore win commissions for some of the plum city housing projects (Kingsborough, Brooklyn, NY, 1940), key civil engineering projects (the highway around the Brooklyn Navy yard, 1941; sections of a parkway and a viaduct for the Triborough Bridge Authority, 1938 and 1940); and significant work within the New York World's Fair in 1939.[10] It was here that the fortunes of Andrews and Skidmore come together.

Andrews was appointed general manager of the New York World's Fair, May 21, 1936. In that position he must have worked closely with Skidmore who soon had special responsibility for the design of a number of pavilions. Andrews left his position with the Fair in the summer of 1938 to become an engineering consultant and opened an office at 30 Rockefeller Plaza, and the first notice of his professional activity thereafter is as a consultant for the Boy Scouts.[11] In 1940 he became the fourth partner and the firm's name was changed again: Skidmore Owings Merrill & Andrews.

Evidence for this new four-person firm is a slender sixteen page typescript entitled "Subject: / File of the Firm of Skidmore, Owings, Merrill & Andrews / Architect-Engineer / New York Chicago." This typescript summary of the firm's work is undated but is probably from late

1941.[12] It lists SOMA's major projects since 1936, their construction costs, and is followed by a series of brief resumés of the main employees. There, in addition to his work on New York parks and the parkway system, Andrews also refers to his work as consulting engineer to the village of Rockville Center, NY; for the Garden City Company, NY; and for Ocean Beach Park Board, New London, CT. Looking through SOMA's list of projects a number are assigned to W. Earle Andrews including significant work for the Triborough Bridge Authority in New York City from 1938 and 1939 before he was appointed in 1940, as the typescript reads, "to head the Civil Engineering Department" (presumably in New York).[13] Others from Moses' operations seem to have been taken in by the new firm at the same time. The typescript lists S. Peter Shumavon as an engineer for the Long Island Park Commission (1930–1934); as head of the design division for the New York Park Commission (1934–38); and as the person "in charge of Engineering Department" (1938 to present) at SOMA.[14] Another Moses associate with ties to SOMA was Ernest J. Clark who worked for the Westchester County Park Com-

mission (1928–30); for the Long Island Park Commission (1930–34); for the New York City Park Department (1934–36); and at the World's Fair (1936–39).[15] After leaving SOMA, Andrews & Clark formed an engineering partnership.[16]

It is hard to escape the conclusion that Skidmore and Owings were interested in W. Earle Andrews because of his close friendship with Robert Moses. SOMA presented itself as an imposing quartet equally balanced between architecture and engineering, equally balanced between New York and Chicago.[17] But was this one case where the ambition of Skidmore and Owings got the better of them? Had they been persuaded to take on Moses' boys by the ever-persuasive Moses against their own best interests as independent operators? Imagine, for a moment, what would the firm looked like had it proceeded forward with that shape? Would design have maintained its strong position at SOMA as it did at SOM? Did the Moses appointees have sufficient sympathy for the architecture that Skidmore and Owings—and certainly Bunshaft—wanted to make? Placing Moses' engineers in the firm in this way would have fixed the hurry-up, earth-moving

Owings, Skidmore, and Merrill at the AIA Gold Medal Ceremony in Washington, DC, 1957

style that Skidmore and Owings both knew from the Century of Progress Exhibition in 1933 and New York in 1939 at the heart of the firm's activities. Would Andrews have remained, a loyal "Moses man," rather than a member of a new entity? Merrill had degrees in engineering and architecture and deep sympathy for architectural design has always been part of the engineering tradition at SOM. SOM in New York never developed its own engineering department. Was this early experience with Andrews one reason for that? Whatever the case, Skidmore and Owings must have decided (or Andrews decided for them) that the fit wouldn't work. By the end of 1941 the firm was back to its holy trinity, Skidmore, Owings & Merrill. Imagining a four-sided Skidmore Owings & Merrill with W. Earle Andrews as the fourth partner underlines the fact that SOM is a design firm first and foremost, and illuminates further the special relationship between engineering and design that has developed at SOM over time. Finally, it reminds us how complicated the issue of balance was in formulating the partnership at the beginning. It may remain just as complicated today.

Acknowledgments: I am grateful for help from SOM partners, including David Childs, Adrian Smith, and Roger Duffy. Thanks also to Louis Skidmore Jr., Houston, TX for permission to quote from the letter files of his father. Karen Widi, librarian at SOM (Chicago), Pam Kane, head, Marketing Division, SOM (Chicago), Elizabeth Kubany, SOM (New York) and Amy Gill, SOM (New York) have also facilitated my work in many important ways for which I am grateful.

[1] Martin Bunzl, "Counterfactual History: A User's Guide," American Historical Review 109 (June 2004), pp. 845−858; Niall Ferguson, ed., Virtual History: Alternatives and Counterfactuals (New York, 1999); Robert Crowley, ed. What If? The World's Foremost Historians Imagine What Might Have Been (New York, 1999).

[2] Nathaniel Alexander Owings, The Spaces in Between: An Architect's Journey (Boston, 1973), p. 67.

[3] Merrill was born in St. Paul, Minnesota and had served in the Artillery Corps during World War I. He had been in practice since 1921 and thus, by comparison with Skidmore and Owings, was relatively well-seasoned. The expectations regarding his ability to find work in the field of housing were not unreasonable. Merrill had been chief zone architect for the Federal Housing Administration (1934−39) and, additionally, had been the associate architect on the Trumbull Park Housing project (1936) and the Winnebago courthouse in Oshkosh, WI (1937). Bunshaft suggests this was the reason he was hired, see Carol Herselle Krinsky, Gordon Bunshaft of Skidmore, Owings & Merrill (New York, 1988), p. 10.

[4] Who's Who in America 33, 1964−1965 (Chicago, 1965).

[5] Andrews states in his resumé, part of a typescript of the commissions and major employees of Skidmore, Owings, Merrill and Andrews ("Subject: File of the Firm of Skidmore, Owings, Merrill & Andrews / Architect-Engineer / New York Chicago," SOM, Chicago, Library, call number 713 1942 Ref) that he was "in direct charge of design and construction of a system of State parks and parkways on Long Island. Projects include Jones Beach, Valley Stream, Sunken Meadow, Wildwood, Heckscher, Belmont, Hither Hills, Montauk, and other parks and Jones Beach, Ocean, Southern Northern, Laurelton, Montauk, and Sunken Meadows Parkways."

[6] Andrews states in "Subject: File of the Firm of Skidmore, Owings, Merrill & Andrews" that he was "Chief Engineer and General Manager- Henry Hudson Parkway Authority during design and construction of high-level arch bridge over Harlem River and parkway connections. Chief Engineer and General Manager- Marine Parkway Authority during design and construction of vertical lift bridge over Rockaway Inlet approaches and connections."

[7] Robert A. Caro, The Power Broker: Robert Moses and the Fall of New York (New York, 1975), p. 1167.

[8] Moses had the key to Andrews' glass-covered swimming pool in Huntington, NY, so that he could stop in for a swim whenever he wanted. See, Caro, p. 813. For information on Paul Moses and Andrews, see Caro, p. 598.

[9] Moses was one of the three speakers at Skidmore's funeral and visited with Eloise Skidmore in Florida after Skidmore's death. Skidmore listed Moses as a reference when he applied for security

clearance from the Department of Defense in 1955, Letter Files, "Registration of Architects Information" (Louis Skidmore Jr. Collection, Houston, TX, Letter files). In 1972, pressed by his critics, Robert Moses wrote to Owings for advice. In his reply Owings wrote: "I am afraid your ears would burn with the compliments inherent in the part you played at the beginning; and more than that, all the way through until your beautiful words at the time of his (Skid's) memorial service." Letter from Owings to Robert Moses, January 11, 1972 (Louis Skidmore Jr. Collection, Houston, TX, Letter files).

[10] The Kingsborough Houses, Brooklyn, were probably built under the direction of J. Walter Severinghaus. Built as a series of blocks in echelon the houses were part of the program for low-cost housing in Brooklyn undertaken by Mayor Fiorello LaGuardia. See the brochure Kingsborough Houses (New York, 1941).

[11] Owings was also a strong supporter of the Boy Scouts of America.

[12] I am very grateful to Adrian Smith who drew my attention to this typescript in the library of SOM (Chicago). For call numbers see note 5.

[13] "Subject: File of the Firm of Skidmore, Owings, Merrill & Andrews," p. 5

[14] Ibid., p. 12.

[15] Ibid., p. 13. .

[16] Andrews and Clark later becomes Bettigole, Andrews & Clark before being taken over by Killam Associates when it is known as BAC Killam Associates. The firm is currently part of Hatch Mott MacDonald. Thanks to Mark O'Connor, counsel to Hatch Mott MacDonald for this information. Telephone interview, March 28, 2005.

[17] In a prospectus for SOM from 1941, after Andrews' departure, John Merrill is described as an "architectural engineer [who] works out of both offices" (i.e., Chicago and New York). In an interview late in his life, Owings was asked about how SOM found partners. His answer was: "Well, one, they cannot be brought in like you buy players from another team. We won't do that. We did it once and it didn't work very well." Was he remembering Andrews? "Interview with Nathaniel Owings," Architecture California 5 (March/April 1983), p. 16.

Scheme 1 of Lake Meadows Housing Development, Chicago, 1950

The Invisible Superblock

Sarah Whiting

Had Skidmore Owings and Merrill's widely published initial scheme for the Lake Meadows housing development on Chicago's Near South Side been built, even Ludwig Hilberseimer, author of those haunting, post-humanist visions of the 1920s, would have been more than a tad nervous.[1] As Ambrose Richardson, SOM's chief of design in Chicago at the time, reminisced, "[It] was a very controversial design. I remember showing it to Hilberseimer, the great urban planner cohort of Mies. He made some comment about it being too big."[2] *Too big for Hilberseimer?* What can that possibly mean? How big is "too big" in Chicago, the city of "big shoulders" and "no little plans"? A description accompanying the project at a 1950 Museum of Modern Art exhibition of SOM's work offers some clues:

Sarah Whiting is an Assistant Professor at Princeton's School of Architecture. She was previously Associate Professor of Architecture at Harvard Graduate School of Design, and she has also taught at the Illinois Institute of Technology, the University of Kentucky, and the University of Florida. Her work focuses on the intersection between space, form, and the subject in the context of 20th-century modernism. Whiting is also a design principal in the architectural firm WW. She was the editor of Ignasi de Sola-Morales' book, Differences: Topographies of Contemporary Architecture; co-editor of Fetish; and the Reviews Editor of Assemblage. Her own writing includes articles in: Eleven Authors in Search of a Building: The Aronoff Center for Design and Art (1996); An Architecture for All Senses: The Work of Eileen Gray (1996); Between War and Peace: Society, Culture and Architecture after World War II (1997); and Mies in America (2001).

This spectacular architectural concept will do much to change the face of the city. To realize the daring arrangement and overwhelming scale of the skyscrapers, try to imagine a single building rising 23 stories straight above a typical New York City street from Fifth to Sixth Avenues. The Chicago skyscraper is almost 200 feet longer than the distance of this city street.[3]

More than a third again the length of a typical New York City block, the project's twenty-three-story building stretched 832 feet long, but was a mere forty feet deep. This slender, extra-long bar was twinned by a second identical bar separated from it by about 1200 feet. Extraordinarily elegant, but somehow unsettling: "too big." This initial superblock scheme, which also included

169

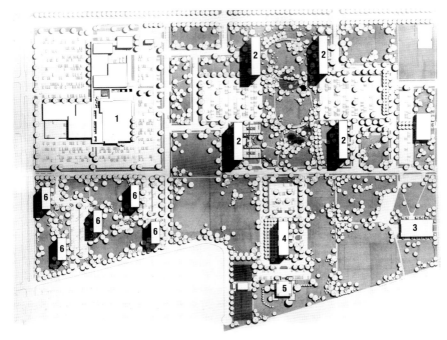

1 Shopping center

2 21-story apartment buildings

3 School

4 13-story apartment building

5 Club building

6 12-story apartment buildings shopping center

Built Scheme, Lake Meadows Masterplan

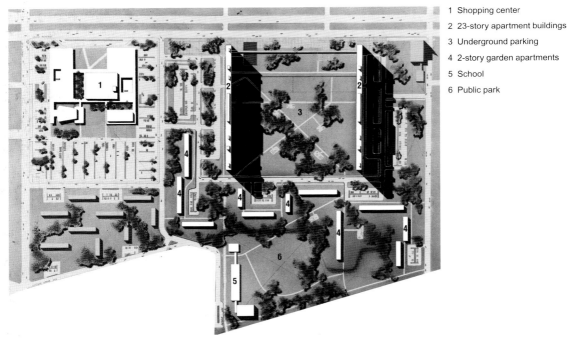

1 Shopping center

2 23-story apartment buildings

3 Underground parking

4 2-story garden apartments

5 School

6 Public park

Scheme 1, Lake Meadows Masterplan

eleven two-story garden apartment bars, a shopping center, a school, church, recreation center, and park, was ultimately replaced by a more conventional proposal built by SOM between 1950 and 1960: ten double loaded corridor slabs of typical dimensions in a reconfigured superblock plan containing those same community amenities.

But was Scheme 1 really *too big?* This original project for Lake Meadows would have entirely rewritten the terms of Chicago urbanism at a scale commensurate with the city's original Jeffersonian platting by constructing *urban thickness* out of *architectural thinness.* The two slender bars defined a crisp, large block of air within the city, whose orthogonality was attuned to the city and whose scale formed a transition between the small fabric of the greystones surrounding the project and the site's big neighbors: Lake Michigan, Daniel Burnham's lakeshore park, and Chicago's endless street grid. Air is made visible by being captured into an abstract block. Between them is a park area with underground parking for 750 cars. A rendering published in the *Chicago Daily News* in July of 1950 shows that block of space barely being held in place by the fragile bars: their scale, combined with the thickened air between them, transforms the massive scale of the entire project into something surprisingly light. Lifted off the ground plane by a glass lobby level, the bars look like sugar wafers precariously balanced on

edge. The aerial perspective of the project, exhibited at MoMA and highlighted in the project's publicity brochures, further underscored Lake Meadows's combination of slenderness and magnitude: one of the bars neatly matches the thin, continuous white line of the infinite street grid that stretches well beyond the perspective's frame to some faraway frontier.

Additional urban delicacy comes from the strategic placing of the short (forty-foot-wide) end of the bars along the street edge, thereby not walling off South Parkway, but rather letting the space of the city slip right through the project to the lake beyond. A letter from Ambrose Richardson to the Federal division of slum clearance and urban redevelopment from July 7, 1950 underscores the importance of not barring the project from the streets that surround it so as not to create a separate enclave.[4] Running east-west in this manner, the buildings permit views of the immediate neighborhood, views of Chicago's skyline, and, most importantly, views of the lake, all while offering each unit the luxury of cross ventilation. The nine-foot wide "gallery in the sky" corridor, would have grille-work and glass, but would have essentially been open air, leading SOM to describe the project as stacked row houses: twenty-three stories of front stoops. In a rendering that accompanied the Chicago Land Clearance Commission's (CLCC) description of the project, the gallery space is shown to

Scheme 1 rendering (inset); photo collage of Scheme 1 as published in the *Chicago Daily News*

be more of a series of outdoor rooms than a corridor—the tiled surface of the apartment exterior takes on a domestic quality, especially when decorated with hanging plants and creating an alcove for a toddler's play pen and a bench and chair ready to accommodate a social gathering.

The rest of the project creates additional urban thickness out of the horizontal ground plane. The shopping center—a second, smaller square of 17.8 acres—is but one story. An early version, shown in the *Chicago Daily News* photo shows the shopping center as having a single, flat, hovering roof, with a cinema/auditorium as an object along the southeast corner. The ensemble of overlapping bars and open spaces creates a dynamic, slightly imbalanced H-shaped shopping center. The CLCC brochure, published the same month as the *Daily News* model photo, however, shows a more conventional shopping center scheme, still an H, but this time a more balanced one with the parking surrounding the building's H with a U-shaped parking grid buffer. It is as if the large program components of the shopping center—the branch department store, super market, and movie theater—had settled down heavily, their size and weight pining down the previously more equalized pinwheeling forms. In a preliminary program statement done by the New York Life Insurance Company (NYLIC), it is noted that the shopping center is important both for "selling" the project to the community at large, but also to "stabilize and insure the overall investment of New York Life Insurance Company in the whole development area."[5]

Combined with the peeling away of the surface to reveal the underground parking at the center of the courtyard separating the two bar buildings, and the horizontal emphasis of the eleven two-story garden apartments, the shopping center contributes to this initial proposal's transformation of the ground plane from mute foundation to active participant.

The delicacy of the two housing bars finds additional echoes in the thin pathways traced over the flat green plain caught between the buildings. The distance of the aerial perspective's viewpoint makes the pathways and the city streets seem almost equal in scale, which domesticates the city's streets by turning them into park paths while simultaneously suggesting that the park is itself a small city, with its own street organization and blocks, not of buildings but of green. The contrast between this delicate tracery of paths and the enormity of the park plain, just like the contrast between the bars' thinness and their size, underscores the project's perpetual oscillation between architecture and urbanism.

Perhaps Hilberseimer's sense that Lake Meadows was "too big" was because this was a plan whose bigness outdid even Burnham. Housing, which would always be relegated to the background as a fabric building in the 1909 Burnham Plan, is here monumentalized into a building that operated at the scale of Chicago's regional landscape, seemingly ignoring the city as it had existed for a hundred years. But Hilberseimer's own contemporaneous plan for the Near South Side (which included the site for Lake Meadows), designed with his students at IIT

Perspective drawing of Scheme 1 23-story apartment buildings

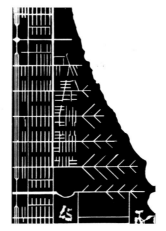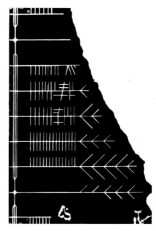

Hilberseimer's plans—initial, intermediate, and final—for Chicago's Near Southside, designed with IIT students in 1952

and published in the "Community Appraisal Study" by the South Side Planning Board in May, 1952, similarly foregrounded housing and was similarly bold in its vision. Hilberseimer proposed to replace the Chicago grid with a fish scale-like street organization (what Albert Pope has referred to as "ladders" in his book of the same name) that would re-orient housing away from the streets (used solely for distribution of people and goods) and toward large communal green spaces that, like Clarence Stein's Garden City plans of the late 1920s, made it possible for children to walk to school without ever crossing a street. Hardly a small vision, Hilberseimer's proposal is presented as a three-phase progression that would eventually entirely replace Chicago's grid with a new

Ludwig Hilberseimer (with pipe) with his IIT students in 1950

order. But his was a big vision at a small scale: like the first SOM proposal for Lake Meadows, Hilberseimer's plan was a combination of low rise row houses and taller towers, but these Y and U shaped towers had small footprints and look from the model photographs to be only about eight to ten stories tall. Like its garden city forebears, the Hilberseimer plan was essentially a suburbanization of the city emphasizing low density housing and replacing the block with an oversized lawn. Lake Meadows was, on the other hand, an intensification of Chicago's urbanity, restructuring the block while maintaining its order.

When Lake Meadows's daring thinness appeared to be too radical to ensure financial backing, the ambition for this intensified urbanscape had to be achieved more by combining an articulated landscape combined with a programmed cityscape rather than through the startling combination of large-scale architecture and urban emptiness that had marked the first scheme. If the initial project put the emphasis on super, the second decidedly placed the stress upon the block. The revised scheme had some variation (five of the double-loaded slabs were twelve stories; another four were twenty-one stories; and the final building—meant to be the slightly higher end one—was a curious thirteen stories in height), but the overall plan was very evenly balanced in terms of building and open space—architecture and urbanism—especially in comparison to the earlier version. Having lost the extraordinary and enormous single open space of the

Perspective drawing of Scheme 1 garden apartments, with 23-story apartments in background

first scheme, the second scheme accentuates smaller, neighborly, semi-public scaled spaces. The project's landscaped pockets—animated by playgrounds and clusters of benches—were carefully defined by curvilinear pathways, small hills, and trees with low canopies. Some of the buildings themselves were similarly broken down in scale: four columns of protruding balconies defined an A-B-A rhythm to the four twenty-one-story buildings; and color and balconies both work to give the thirteen-story building an A-B-C-B-A rhythm.

Despite the first scheme's emphasis on the great cube of open space, it is possible to trace Lake Meadows's landscaping strategy of defining these semi-public zones as early as the project's conception. In several letters to SOM in 1949, General Otto Nelson, NYLIC's Vice President in Charge of Housing (and army buddy of South Side Planning Board member Fred Kramer, who was instrumental in attracting NYLIC to invest in Lake Meadows and whose real estate firm, Draper and Kramer were—and still are—the project's rental agents) consistently underscored the value that landscape brought to the project. Recognizing that the site was especially well located near Chicago's greatest natural asset—Lake Michigan—Nelson recommended "pulling in the lake front to bring its influence to bear on every part of the project." Nelson also judiciously understood that the project was groundbreaking as the first redevelopment project and that it was important to set a good precedent,

Nelson stressed that the project be understood as semi-public; by welcoming public access, it could become a community-wide asset and have an even greater and more rapid influence on the whole Near South Side. Nelson suggested that landscaping be employed to create more private (and controlled) areas, such as children's play areas: "This can probably be accomplished by the judicious use of grading features, berms, landscaping, fencing, placement of buildings and visual control by project staff." In a letter a year later, Ambrose Richardson took Nelson's implication even further, suggesting that landfill could help the row houses gain desirable lake front views, and would, more importantly, also "serve as a psychological fence from the casual nuisances."[7] But the five twelve-story buildings, which were the first to be completed, have no articulation to their facades and little variation in the green spaces that separate them, suggesting that either a change in design attitude at SOM (as documented by Nicholas Adams in his study of SOM, the project changed hands several times over the course of its design and construction), or a client reaction to the urban effect of the first cluster of buildings led to the fulfillment of Nelson's early vision of a semi-public project.[8]

In addition to entwining a series of designers at SOM— among others, Ambrose Richardson, Walter Netsch, James Scheeler, and Gertrude Kerbis—the story threads of both Lake Meadows versions interweave architecture, urbanism, legislation, public relations, personalities, and—to quote British architectural historian Christopher Woodward—some "creepy social engineering" that worked to obscure the project from history's limelight.[9] Lake Meadows's history stretches back to June, 1946 when two institutions—the Illinois Institute of Technology and Michael Reese Hospital—joined forces to spur the redevelopment of the Near South Side of Chicago by founding the South Side Planning Board (SSPB), an unofficial group of citizen planners that also included Chicago businessmen, academics, and community leaders. Astonishingly well structured, ambitious, and productive—especially given that it was a volunteer organization—the SSPB put forth a comprehensive vision for the redevelopment of a seven-square-mile area and became a significant liaison between the city and the entire South Side.[10]

Exactly one year after the founding of the SSPB, Illinois passed the Blighted Areas Redevelopment and Relocation Acts, which paved the way for the federal Housing Act of 1949 by legislating measures for slum clearance and urban renewal. Attesting that "neither the demolition nor repair of an occasional building changes the character of a blighted neighborhood," these Illinois Acts made the acquisition of large parcels of land available through purchase by the Chicago Land Clearance Commission, the powers of eminent domain, and "the use of public funds to squeeze the water out of the inflated values of land and structures."[11] This legislation thoroughly transformed the dynamics of urban development in Chicago and ultimately served as a model for subsequent federal legislation that would enable large-scale urban-renewal projects throughout the country during the 1950s.[12]

Within days of the passage of the Blighted Areas Acts, "six private and public organizations concerned with the rebuilding of a slum area," who were clearly anticipating the legislation's approval, published a sixty-two-page, carefully researched and professionally designed booklet entitled *An Opportunity for Private and Public Investment in Rebuilding Chicago*. A collaboration of IIT, Michael Reese, the South Side Planning Board, the Metropolitan Housing Council, Pace Associates, and the Chicago Housing Authority, *An Opportunity* laid out a redevelopment plan "at the cost of a battleship"—an appropriate analogy for the postwar economy. Organized under the guidance of Walter Blucher, Executive Director of the American Society of Planning Officials (based in Chicago) and Walter Gropius (who was then Chairman of the Department of Architecture at Harvard), the joint redevelopment plan, which called for high population densities but low land coverage, was clearly influenced by the Congress of International Architcture's (CIAM) tower in the park ambitions. Even at this early date, the site for Lake Meadows—101 acres just south of Michael Reese Hospital along Lake Michigan—was reserved for high rise housing and a large shopping center.

Although the famously endless Chicago grid was respected in the Rebuilding Chicago proposal, it was nonetheless loosened, according to the CLCC: "redevelopment should change the outmoded street pattern and provide open spaces for grass and trees, parks and playgrounds."[13] Despite the CCLC's lack of enthusiasm for the Chicago grid, the South Side Plan demonstrated that Chicago's orthogonal street plan was

"...AT THE COST OF A BATTLESHIP"

From *An Opportunity for Private and Public Investment in Rebuilding Chicago*, 1947 hardly outmoded but was in fact elastic enough to absorb superblock planning.

Platted in 1830, Chicago was squarely set within the gridiron tradition systematized by Thomas Jefferson's 1785 Northwest Ordinance, which subdivided the Western Territories into townships of thirty-six square miles. This grid system divided the landscape into commodifiable parcels, thereby facilitating rapid (and rampant) land speculation. The grid homogenized the landscape in such a way that the cityscape was liberated, unanchored from its ground. Whereas earlier examples of landownership turned a deed or a title into a metaphoric stake in the earth, in Chicago and other Western cities, land became paper thin, as if each plot were but randomly dealt chances in an interminable, rapid paced game of Texas Hold'em. The writer James Silk Buckingham's hyperbolic description from the early 1830s provides a telling glimpse of the city's speculative whirlwind: "some lots changed hands ten times in a single day and the 'evening purchaser' paid at least 'ten times as much as the price paid by the morning buyer for the same spot!"[14] Such land division multiplied profits. The redundant, repetitive exchange of plots depended upon the assumption that the city's platted rectangles were both easily identifiable and interchangeable. Accordingly, the plots were numbered and, throughout the city's first real estate boom of 1836 were sold sight-unseen in auction houses in New York, oftentimes offering surprises to the owners when they eventually made their way to the city named by the Indians for its unpleasant smells.[15]

Despite the implied rigor of the ordinance grid's mathematical definition, Chicago's blocks have never been entirely homogeneous: the standard (or usual) Chicago block is 266 by 600 feet.[16] The word "usually," oft repeated within the pages of *The Manual of Surveying Instructions* of 1947, suggests regularity but admits aberration. If New York's unyielding grid "forces Manhattan's builders to develop a new system of formal values, to invent strategies for the distinction of one block from another," Chicago's is essentially the opposite: the grid itself is manipulated in order to distinguish one project from another.[17] The SSPB Plan replaced Chicago's dense blocks with half-mile-square (2640 by 2640 feet— suddenly 832 feet seems quite reasonable) superblocks with permeable perimeters, thereby maintaining public

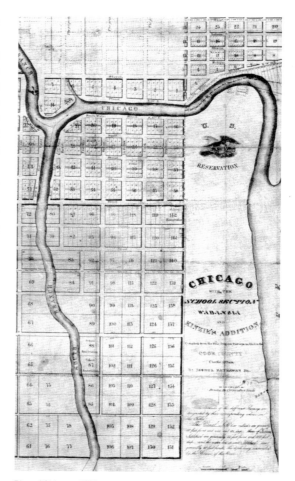

Plan of Chicago, 1834

accessibility—sometimes visual and sometimes physical—across the Plan's entire seven-square-mile area. In keeping with the model initiated with the IIT campus plan that preceded the South Side Plan, the ratios of footprint to ground plane were kept low, leaving large, open, landscaped areas for pedestrian and recreation use. Higher building heights allowed planners to create open space while still accommodating the necessary population densities, although the plan never aspired to replicate the extreme population density of the housing that it replaced.[18] Unlike earlier modern examples of superblock planning, the figured fields of the envisioned South Side Plan mixed densities, programs, and heights in order to diversify the urban experience of the block.

Within the South Side Plan, Lake Meadows was the first project to be developed under the auspices of the new Illinois legislation. The CLCC acquired and cleared the land of its 741 residential structures (originally containing 1,127 dwelling units; by 1949, these had been divided to create 2,782 units), and then sold it at cost to the New York Life Insurance Company.[19] The project was developed as an integrated, middle-class development.[20] Most of the low-income residents displaced by the project were relocated to the 800-unit Dearborn Homes, a Chicago Housing Authority project located immediately north of the IIT campus; once cleared, the Lake Meadows site became a tabula rasa landfill within the dense Chicago grid.

As described in a *New York Times* article of 1950, SOM's original scheme for Lake Meadows "would appear like two big blades knifing into Chicago's skyline."[21] While the scale of this analogy is so large as to suggest a mythical tale, the force of the image is startling in an article of otherwise mere reportage: are the knives indicative of the violence of the crime-ridden slums? Are they references to the "surgical operations" on what many planning periodicals referred to as the area's "cancerous slums"? Or are they part of a magic act—a miraculous trans-formation of the South Side that would be no less incredible than pulling a rabbit out of a hat or sawing the magician's assistant in two?

Lake Meadows's "two big blades" and super scaled block were cast in positive terms through the project's design, revisions, and construction—it was featured at the MoMA exhibition on SOM in 1950; referred to in both the popular and architectural press; and it has always, even to this day, been lauded as a progressive, integrated project and a well-maintained, desirable housing development. Nevertheless, Lake Meadows has also had a curiously invisible presence on the horizon of America's—or even Chicago's—housing history. Its role in ushering in urban renewal legislation surely plays a role in this invisibility but its siting on the Near South Side and its African American constituency surely present even more significant factors. Furthermore, as the superblock currently undergoes renewed reviling from both the left and right following the destruction of the World Trade Center on September 11, 2001, and as numerous public housing projects within the Near South Side are destroyed in an effort to find a quick fix for what is a much, much deeper problem than architecture, I would argue that Lake Meadows runs the risk of being swept in

Aerial of built scheme

the tide of criticism against the modernist superblock. While the as-built project did not advance Chicago's urbanism in the ways that its more daring predecessor might have, Lake Meadows both expands and augments Chicago's elastic grid socially, economically, politically, and architecturally. The superblock was hardly the urban superhero that its proponents envisioned in the 1940s and 50s, but its short history, exemplified by projects like Lake Meadows, offers an important glimpse into the recent history of America's urban realm that might keep us from rendering the superblock's promise invisible.

2005 view of built scheme 21-story apartment buildings

1 I would like to thank Nicholas Adams for his generous help with my research on Lake Meadows. I would additionally like to thank Karen Widi and Philip Enquist of SOM Chicago for their assistance, and Scott Duncan SOM New York for inviting me to write this piece and then for his patience long after doing so. This research forms part of my forthcoming book *Superblockisms*, which examines the history and execution of the Near South Side plan in the 1940s and 50s in Chicago.

2 *Oral History of Ambrose M. Richardson*, interviewed by Betty J. Blum (Chicago, 1990), p. 168.

3 *Exhibition of Recent Buildings by Skidmore, Owings and Merrill*, MoMA September 26 – November 5, 1950, p. 14.

4 Ambrose Richardson letter to Mr. N. S. Keith, Director Division of Slum Clearance and Urban Redevelopment, Washington, DC, July 7, 1950 in SOM archives.

5 *Program for Planning Redevelopment Area #1 South Side Chicago*, Illinois New York Life Insurance Company, p. 10.

6 General Otto Nelson to SOM Planning Staff, July 13, 1949, p. 3.

7 Richardson letter to Keith, op.cit., p. 2.

8 See Nicholas Adams's forthcoming book on SOM.

9 Christopher Woodward, *Skidmore Owings and Merrill* (NY, 1970), p. 12. Woodward notes that "were it not for the creepy social engineering involved, [the first Lake Meadows project] would have eclipsed the achievement of the [Smithson's] later housing at Park Hill, Sheffield, England (built 1955–1961)."

10 The most comprehensive story behind the formation of the South Side Planning Board can be found in Shirley Werthamer's Masters Thesis, *Private Planning for Urban Development: The South Side Planning Board of Chicago 1947*, Department of Political Science, University of Chicago 1947.

11 John McKinlay, Chairman, Chicago Land Clearance Commission, *Redevelopment Project Number 1: A Report to the Mayor and the City Council of the City of Chicago and to the Illinois State Housing Board* (March 1949), pp. 5–6.

12 A diagram, replete with dynamic arrows denoting fast action, depicts the process underwritten by the act: based on information gathered via surveys and studies, the Chicago Land Clearance Commission (CLCC) determined what properties should be condemned and how they should be redeveloped, subject to the approval of the City Council and the State Housing Board. Reflecting a Keynesian influence, the CLCC's powers of land acquisition, tenant relocation, demolition, construction, and sale were funded by city bond issues and money allocated from the state; federal support was included after the Federal Housing Act was passed in 1949.

13 McKinlay, Redevelopment Project Number 1: A Report to the Mayor, p. 5.

14 James Silk Buckingham, *The Eastern and Western States of America* (London, 1842), as cited in John Reps, *The Making of Urban America* (Princeton, 1965), p. 302.

15 "Historians still argue over the origin of the name, some maintaining it comes from the Indian Chicagou, 'garlic,' while others hold that it was derived from Shegagh, or 'skunk.' There is general agreement, however, that the odors of the place were dreadful and that the Indians were correct in referring to it as "the place of the evil smell." Reps 1965, p. 300.

16 Homer Hoyt, *One Hundred Years of Land Values in Chicago: The Relationship of the Growth of Chicago to the Rise in Its Land Values 1830–1933* (Chicago, 1933), pp. 428–429.

17 Rem Koolhaas, *Delirious New York* (New York, 1984), pp. 20–21.

18 "The percentage of building coverage in the area [Near South Side before redevelopment] is 31% of the net buildable area (not including streets, alleys, and sidewalks), which is almost twice the percentage for the city as a whole." McKinlay, Redevelopment Project Number 1: A Report to the Mayor, p. 14.

19 John McKinlay, Chairman, CLCC, Redevelopment Project No. 1: A Second Report, *The New York Life Insurance Company Redevelopment Plan* (July 1950), pp. 10–18. According to the CLCC Progress Report of 1955 (Chicago, 1955), "Of the 725 parcels in the area, 562 were obtained by negotiation" (10), which suggests that the other 163 were obtained via forcible eviction.

20 In an interview conducted with Fred Kramer, November 20, 1998, I was struck at how committed he was to Lake Meadows's integrated status and how frustrated he was at how difficult it was to keep it at the desired 50-50 integration level because Caucasians were reluctant to live there. This integrated vision had direct effects upon the design, as noted by Nicholas Adams (op.cit.) who explains that the project originally was designed to have a swimming pool, but the vision of African Americans and Caucasians swimming together was too radical and was replaced by the less intimate leisure facilities of the tennis court and skating rink.

21 "Chicago Housing for 100 Acres Cited as a Model of Planning," *New York Times*, October 8, 1950, p. 1.

Project Credits

Creative & Performing Arts High School
Camden, New Jersey
Designed 2003–04

Client
New Jersey Schools Construction Corporation
Collaborating artist
Robert Whitman
Design Partner
Roger Duffy
Managing Partner
Anthony Vacchione
Educational Design Specialist
Walter Smith
Project Manager
Chris McCready
Senior Designer
Sven Schroeter
Sr. Technical Coordinator
Michael Carline
Technical Coordinator
Peter Cho
Team Members
Michael Bardin, I-Ching Katie Lee, Dongkyu Lee, Simone Pfeiffer, Karen Seong
Assistant Project Manager
David Yanks
Structural Engineering
Consulting Engineers Collaborative, Inc.
Mechanical Engineering
Concord Engineering Group, Inc.
Landscape Architect
MKW + Associates, LLC
Geotechnical Engineering
Powell-Harpstead, Inc.
Civil Engineering
Armand Corporation
Information Technology
Intertech Associates, Inc.

Office Building Schlosshotel
Velden am Worthersee, Austria
Designed 2003

Client
Schlosshotel
Design Partner
Larry Oltmanns
Managing Partner
Mark Regulinski
Senior Designer
Duncan Swinhoe
Team Members
George Arvanitis, Duncan Bainbridge, Pieter Coetzee, Coco Cugat, Olaf Detering, Tesoc Hah, Richard Haigh, Isabelle Hanig, Timo Kujala, Lawrence Lerr, Lorena Prieto, Kaaren Rutherford, Louise Sullivan
Project Manager
Ed Guerra
Structural Engineering
Matt Houson
Mechanical Engineering
Arup, Mohsen Zikri
Technical Coordinator
Matthias Schobert

Pin-Fuse Joint™
Designed 2002
Patent awarded 2004

Structural Design Partner
Mark Sarkisian
Structural Team Members
Shea Bond, Jean-Pierre Chakar,
Rupa Garai, Eric Long,
Neville Mathias, Jun Racines,
Collaborating Team Member
Gregory Deierlein, Stanford University

ARB Bank Headquarters
Riyadh, Saudi Arabia
Designed 2003–04

Client
Al Rajhi Bank
Design Partner
Gary Haney
Managing Partner
Peter Magill
Senior Designer
Aybars Asci
Team Members
Devawong Devakul, Joyce Ip, Yasemin
Kologlu, Noppon Pisutharnon
Project Manager
Karim Musfy

**United States Air Force Academy
Cadet Chapel**
Colorado Springs, Colorado
Designed 1954

Partner in Charge
Nathanial Owings
Director
John O. Merrill
Partner in Charge of Design
Gordon Bunshaft
General Manager
A.-Carroll L. Tyler
Partner in Charge of Chicago Office
William Hartman
Director of Design
Walter Netsch
Director of Production/Contracting
J. Train
Director of Engineering
Edward O. Merrill
Design Team
Stanley Allan, Stanislaw Gladych, John F.
Hartray, John Hoops, Gertrude Lempp
Kerbis, Carl Kohle, Al Lockett, Roger
Margerum, Mitsuru Otsuji, Gertrude
Peterhaus, Louis Rocah, William Rouzie,
Otto Stark, Bob Ward, George Wickstead,
Ralph Youngren
Production Team
Karl C. Anderson, A. J. Brown, A. J.
Delong, Sam Sachs
Engineering Team
Henry L. Conger

**US Air Force Academy Cadet Chapel
Restoration**
Colorado Springs, Colorado
Designed 2003–04

Client
United States Air Force Academy
Design Partner
Gary Haney
Technical & Managing Partner
Carl Galioto
Team Members
Michael Carline, Jeffrey Feingold, Donald
Marmen, Karen Seong, David Yanks,
Teresa Zix
Project Manager
Nazila Shabestari
Structural Consultant
SOM Chicago—Charles Besjak
Mechanical Consultant
SOM Chicago—Noriel Nicholas, Varkie
Thomas
Technical Coordinator
Scott Yocom
Exterior Envelope Consultant
Heintges Consultants
Environmental Consultant
Maxim Technologies
Cost Estimating Consultant
Hanscomb Faithful & Gould
Inspection Consultant
Robert Heintges

Image Credits

Acknowledgment

The Partners of SOM extend their thanks to all those who contributed to the represented work. We would also like to thank Nancy Cheung, Scott Duncan, Colin Franzen, Kai Hotson, Yasemin Koluglu, Eric Long, Vanessa Paulsen, Paul Preissner, David Yanks, and SOM librarian Susan Lane for assistance in assembling, writing, and coordinating the materials for this *Journal 4*.

Edited by
Diane Ghirardo

Associate editor
Megan Feehan

SOM Journal coordinator
Amy Gill

Editorial coordination
Tas Skorupa

Copyediting
Eugenia Bell

Design and typesetting
SOM with Ines Weber

Typeface
Arial MT

Paper
Nopacoat matt

Binding
Nething Buchbinderei GmbH & Co. KG,
Weilheim / Teck

Reproductions and printing
Dr. Cantz'sche Druckerei, Ostfildern

© 2006 Hatje Cantz Verlag, Ostfildern,
and authors

Published by
Hatje Cantz Verlag
Zeppelinstrasse 32
73760 Ostfildern
Germany
Tel. +49 711 4405-0
Fax +49 711 4405-220
www.hatjecantz.com

Hatje Cantz books are available internationally at selected bookstores and from
the following distribution partners:

USA/North America – D.A.P., Distributed
Art Publishers, New York,
www.artbook.com
UK – Art Books International, London,
www.art-bks.com
Australia – Tower Books, Frenchs Forest
(Sydney), www.towerbooks.com.au
France – Interart, Paris, www.interart.fr
Belgium – Exhibitions International,
Leuven, www.exhibitionsinternational.be
Switzerland – Scheidegger, Affoltern am
Albis, www.ava.ch

For Asia, Japan, South America, and
Africa, as well as for general questions,
please contact Hatje Cantz directly at
sales@hatjecantz.de, or visit our home-
page www.hatjecantz.com for further
information.

ISBN-10: 3-7757-1803-6
ISBN-13: 9-783-7757-1803-5

Printed in Germany

Cover illustration
Hilton Hotel, Istanbul, 1955 (photograph:
Ezra Stoller / ESTO)